PALMS & PEARLS

OR

SCENES IN CEYLON

KANDY LAKE FROM THE TEMPLE OF THE SACRED TOOTH.

PALMS & PEARLS

OR

SCENES IN CEYLON

ALAN WALTERS

ISBN : 978-93-5324-509-2 (HB)
First Published, London, 1892
Published, 2020
Published by
Facsimile Publisher
12 Pragati Market
Ashok Vihar, Ph-2
Delhi-110052
E-mail: books@facsimilepublisher.com

Printed at: G. Print Process, Delhi.

Palms & Pearls or Scenes in Ceylon

Author: Alan Walters

PALMS & PEARLS

OR

SCENES IN CEYLON

BY

ALAN WALTERS

LONDON
RICHARD BENTLEY & SON, NEW BURLINGTON STREET
Publishers in Ordinary to Her Majesty the Queen
1892

Aut ubi Taprobanen Indica cingit aqua.

OVID *ex Pont.* i. v. 80.

I see Aladdin in his cave,
I follow Sinbad on the shore.

. . . .

E'en now I feel my spirit yearn,
Not as the stranger of a day,
Who soon forgets where late he dwelt—
But as a friend who, far away,
Feels even what at first he felt.

TO

ROBERT LOUIS STEVENSON

THE

ENCHANTER OF THE NEW ARABIAN NIGHTS

WHO BY HIS MAGIC ART

HAS LONG SINCE WON THE

PALM

AND WHOSE NAME HERE WRITTEN

IS THE ONLY DISTINCTION OF THESE MEMORIES OF THE

ISLE OF SINBAD :

TO THE

STRONG SWIMMER

WHO OUT AMONG THE RACING BILLOWS

HAS DIVED AND BROUGHT UP MANY A

PEARL

FOR THE ENRICHING AND THE DELIGHT OF MEN :

THIS PEBBLE FROM A SUNNY SHORE

IS OFFERED WITH AFFECTIONATE RESPECT

BY A

WADER IN THE SHALLOWS

CONTENTS

PALMS AND PEARLS

CHAPTER I

INTRODUCTORY

THE following pages are the outcome of a sojourn in Ceylon, during which I had more opportunities than fall to the lot of the ordinary traveller of becoming acquainted with its many beauties, and of observing the daily life and customs of its people.

Says one man: "Ceylon is a place to be shunned. Loathsome leeches, deadly snakes, repulsive insects, predatory crocodiles, blood-thirsty sharks, make life a burden by land and sea; for three months of the year you are grilled, and during the other nine you live in an atmosphere like the steam over a dyer's vat; rice and curry for tiffin, and curry and rice for dinner; the natives are cheats, atheists, and devil-worshippers; to-day you dine with your friend, and to-morrow you bury him; none but a fool would live in Ceylon."

Says another: "Ceylon is a paradise upon earth. Rightly does the Mohammedan affirm that heaven is but forty miles distant, only he might with equal truth have put it nearer; hundreds of miles of coffee with its fragrant flowers and its ruddy fruit; thousands of acres of the most delicious tea; every climate that man desires, from 60° to 140°; magnificent landscape and forest scenery; glorious festoons of graceful creepers, aromatic shrubs, gorgeous flowers; the glades bright with flashing birds and butterflies; the rivers spangled with gems and gold; on its shores the goodliest pearls of the merchantman; the nights superb, the days a long dream of delight; the people gentle and without guile; here are you without any exertion master of every luxury."

The truth, as usual, lies in the mean; and it is my purpose to give in a plain way such an idea of Ceylon as will enable my readers to steer between the two extremes, and to form a just opinion of the wonders of an island with which are associated some of the most pleasant memories of my own life.

First, as to climate. Colombo is commonly said to be the hottest city in the Queen of England's dominions. The casual visitor will feel no surprise at the absence of chimney-pots, for which, as for tailors, there is little need in a city of which the mean annual temperature is 81° Fahrenheit. The average rainfall is 95 inches—half that of Zanzibar, and nearly four times that of London. Kandy gets considerably more rain than Colombo, Trincomalee and the east coast much less, while on the Malabar coast, but a few miles to the north-west, a fall of 13 inches in twenty-four hours is not unknown. In Colombo the hottest months are April and May, the coolest January and December.

It cannot be denied that at least in the coastal and low-lying parts the climate of Ceylon is not productive of any extraordinary physical energy. For weeks at a time earth and sky and sea lie wrapt in a soft and sensuous calm, suggestive of the tranquil existence of the Lotus-eaters, or the swoon-like repose of the Seven Sleepers. The sea of purest sapphire lies shimmering under a blaze of sunshine, which bathes every object in a burnish of gold. The wave has hardly energy enough to dandle the fisherman's canoe, or to cream with snowy foam the yellow strip of sand, which parts it from the flower-spangled grass and the clusters of bending palms. Here and there the sparkle of the waters is streaked with shafts of light, that tell of shallows whose golden sands blend divinely with the blue of heaven. All nature lies as in a voluptuous dream, while over all bends lovingly a dome of azure reflecting its glowing splendours on the nether world, or dulled by a mellow haze as of woven air rather than vulgar atmosphere. For in Ceylon, as in other equatorial lands, the strength of the light is so great that objects are either too sharply defined or else blurred in a quivering blaze. There are lacking those glorious depths of colouring and that gentle softness of outline which lend such beauty to the highlands of Scotland and the fjords of Norway. The beauty of the tropics is beauty that lacks sublimity; all is so soft and smiling that there is wanting the power to stir the springs of thought or breed ideas within the brain. The luxuriant growth on every side has a certain oppressive effect, which is intensified by an excess of damp heat, and by an abnormal proportion of that carbon which, favourable to vegetable, is distinctly deleterious to animal life.[1]

On the occasion of my first landing in the tropics I well remember how I used to revel in the light and heat and the glories of the floral world. But after a while this feeling began to evaporate. There was something too aristocratic about the gorgeous blossoms and flowering trees. I began to long for the sight of a bluebell, or a primrose, or a forget-me-not. Notwithstanding all its glories, tropical vegetation never wears an English spring look; there is no green and gold of daffodils, nor sheen of buttercups, nor glory of summer iris, nor peeping crocus. There is a certain cloying permanent sameness, which leaves one strangely unsatisfied; the charm of freshness is lost in the multitude of evergreens, which keep up driblets of bloom all the year round. The tropics can boast indeed of a plethora of dazzling charm; but what Englishman in Ceylon or Fiji has not longed sometimes for a whiff of the wall-

[1] Note A.

flower that scented the old garden at home? English flowers have a more sociable look somehow.

There is a derangement of the physical system no less than of the mental by the heat of the tropics. Through relaxation of the cellular tissue much of its contractile power is lost, and as a natural result the defective lymphatic circulation makes the healing of wounds and bruises a tedious process. The nervous system often gets irritable, and the slightest hurt if neglected may give trouble.

The traveller who may chance to arrive friendless in Ceylon, and whose only object is to see the island, must prepare himself for the loss of many things in the manner of his daily life. Except in one or two of the towns, hotels, in the proper sense of the word, are conspicuous by their absence. Buildings called "rest-houses" are maintained by Government, in which at a fixed tariff the wayfarer is supplied with the bare necessaries of life. But beyond those he must depend usually upon his own resources.

He must learn not to turn up his nose at such occasional viands as bats, bees, beetles, cuttlefish, or the eggs of the sea-urchin. If he asks for mutton, he must not be perturbed if he gets pickled monkey, which, I can assure him, is by no means bad. Snakes and iguanas, and the multitudinous mysteries of mongrel curries, will now and again try his patience, and possibly his digestion. I do not mean that such dishes will be found in the *ménus* of the Grand Oriental Hotel at Colombo. But even there, where the best that can be procured is put upon the table, the butcher's meat will be considered poor, with the exception of Jaffna mutton. Turkeys, guinea-fowl, pea-fowl, and pigeons may all be eaten thankfully and with relish, as also the small brown goose. Ducks are not recommended, but the poultry as a rule is good, saving only the black-boned specimens called *kalu maskulalo.* Mulligatawny soup (Tamul, *milagu tannir* = pepper-water) is better made in Colombo than anywhere else on earth; to which I may add that the pork, although of excellent flavour, is sometimes so red as to warrant the idea that the pig had been fed on geraniums in order to improve the hams.

It does not do to inquire too closely into the mysteries of oriental cookery. A gentleman was strolling past his kitchen one morning in India, and was surprised to find his cook using one of his socks for a coffee strainer. The man promptly confessed his misdeed, but assured his master that he would not have taken it had it not been a dirty one.

A lady made up her mind to give out no more pudding cloths, as she found that they invariably disappeared. One day when there was a delay in serving up the sweets she visited the scene of action, and found the cook in a state of nudity boiling the pudding in one end of his waist-cloth. Another lady's taste for bread and butter pudding was suddenly annihilated by her finding the cook one day squatting on the ground with a large lump of butter stuck on the end of his big toe, from which he was rapidly spreading slices of bread for his mistress's pudding. From which the moral is: judge of what is put on the table by its present merits rather than by its possible antecedents.

Of course to a stranger armed with a letter of introduction that will open the door of a bungalow to him life will be a different affair. The hospitality of the Ceylon merchants and planters is proverbial, and a sojourn upon a tea or coffee estate is an experience to be looked back upon with feelings of the utmost pleasure. Many of the hill bungalows are situated in the heart of grand scenery. I lived for some time in one which stood high up opposite the rolling patanas or grasslands of the fine Great Western range. It was a stone-built dwelling of one storey, with the usual deep verandahs and cool airy rooms, hemmed in by masses of bamboo, eucalyptus, rhododendron, convolvuli, roses, and a thousand other flowery beauties. The scene was one never to be forgotten. How often did I gaze upon it, and look forward with dread to the time when I should have once more to face the din and unrest of cities!

Above all, how glorious were the early mornings. Step out with me on to the verandah, while the Appo or "boy" is still sleeping peacefully upon his palm-mat outside my door. Not a sound is to be heard in this calm hour before dawn except far down below the distant tinkling of the Kotmallé Ganga, as it babbles along its stony bed on its swift course to Kandy. The air is heavy with scent of lilies and roses and champacs. The dewdrops gleam like pearls upon the tips of the rose-pink bougainvilleas. As we stand and watch the serene beauty of slumbering nature, the stars grow pale, the first quivering rays of the sun shoot up their golden shafts to the zenith, and tip the gaudy hollyhock trees. Now a saucy squirrel peeps at us from among the gay plumes of yonder acacia; a dayal with rich clear note pipes "good-morrow" to the world; a green lizard glides past hastening betimes to his breakfast; with great suddenness the day comes; the "rosy-fingered morn" has small resting-place in the tropics; swiftly does Night shrink back from the first kiss of the god of day.

Nor less to be remembered were the evenings. One such by the edge of the sea I can never forget. I had strolled out towards the setting of the sun to enjoy the deep diapason of the waves, like no other sound in nature, as they break over the reefs of coral. There before me was the sea, stretching with its many-twinkling smile to the Antarctic circle, and lying like a mirror of burnished metal, save where along its margin the surf rose and fell flashing like a girdle of silver. The evening was coming on apace; the palms were aglow with bars of light, and over the water long shadows lay streaming like weeds or tresses of sleeping mermaidens. I left the strand, and after wandering a few hundred yards found my path stopped by the dense jungle growth. But what a scene was before me! Across a little valley, hung with nature-woven tapestry of ferns and clambering vines, there glittered a tiny cascade like a jewelled pendant on the bosom of a white cliff. At its foot there was a flashing, as if handfuls of diamond dust were being flung athwart the sunbeams, while across it hung a strip of rainbow, like a torn many-hued banneret. On every side were streaming "cataracts of leaves" breaking into a foaming wealth of blossom. Overhead there sailed across the sky a stately snow-white bird, silent and solitary as a silver meteor.

I lingered until the light began to die. One moment the western sky was deluged in blood-red glory, the sea was as amber, the shore as antique gold; the next, a purple twilight lay over all, and the sky was already giving back earth's blossoms in countless star-clusters, of which some laid a mimic track of fire along the surface of the sea. Then I turned and went back by the jungle, under groves of ghostly palms, where vines ran riot, intermarried with the flaming ginger and climbing rattans, and the night-blowing cereus was opening its ivory urn to greet the coming moonbeams. As I drew near to the village the soft strange song of girls, and a wisp of bluest smoke curling here and there through the feathery trees towards the stars, told me that I was still on earth.

CHAPTER II

HISTORY

CEYLON, the Pearl of the Orient, which lies in the broad bosom of the Indian Ocean like a bright spring leaf, may be truly called an island of romance, the mere name of which calls up memories of pearls and palms, elephants and cinnamon, rubies and aromas. Thither, 2000 years ago, across the long billows came the Arabian merchant from the Persian Gulf, and cast his wooden anchor alongside the Malay from Sunda and the Chinaman from far Cathay. Here it was that some of the fascinating adventures of Sinbad took place, who, armed with a letter from the Khaleef to the King of Serendib, embarked at Bussora, and found in Ceylon a welcome at the court of a prince who commanded his adventures to be written in letters of gold and laid up in the archives of his kingdom.[1]

[1] Note B.

Some tell us that here was the Tarshish of the ancient Phœnicians. Without entering into so vexed and conjectural a question, about which too much has been written for it ever to be satisfactorily decided, I may mention that if you ask a Tamul coolie to-day the name of an ape or a peacock, he will give you the very same words as were known to the old inspired Hebrew writers.

In the *Eireks Saga*, an Icelandic narrative of the fourteenth century, probably a Christian recension of an old heathen myth, we have the adventures of a Norwegian, who vowed that he would find out the Deathless Land of which mention was made in his mythology. He made his way to India and journeyed for many days through a dense forest, at the other end of which he came out upon a narrow piece of water dividing the mainland from Paradise, none other than Ceylon, "most beautiful, and the grass as gorgeous as purple, studded with flowers and traversed by many rills. The sun shone cloudless without night or darkness; the calm of the air was great and breathed redolent with odours of blossoms."

By some the island was included in the

realms of that very mythical personage Prester John. The Hereford map (thirteenth century) puts Paradise as a circular isle near India, cut off from the continent not only by the sea, but also by a battlemented wall with a gateway to the west. It is to the same locality that Hugo Victor alludes in his *De Situ Terrarum*, when he says that "Paradise is a spot in the orient productive of all kinds of woods and pomiferous trees: it contains the Tree of Life; there is neither cold nor heat [*sic*], but perpetual equable temperature."

6700 miles from the mouth of the Thames, by way of the Suez Canal, lies the fair isle, within the tropic of Cancer, between 5° 53′ and 9° 51′ N. latitude, and 79° 42′ and 81° 55′ E. longitude. In extent it is 266 miles long by 140 wide, covering an area of 25,365 square miles (of which about one-fifth is under cultivation), thus being one-sixth less than Ireland, and equalling Holland and Belgium put together.

Divided from the mainland of India by a narrow channel unnavigable by sea-going ships, many have supposed that at one period Ceylon formed part of the continent of Asia. The

Singhalese have a tradition that at some remote time the island was joined to a vast tract known in the mystical epics of the Brahmans as Lanka, stretching southwards beyond the equator, and on either hand from Africa to Cathay. Such a theory, as Sir Emerson Tennent points out, is not at variance with the discoveries of geology, since there is little doubt that, whereas at the beginning of the Tertiary period the whole of northern Asia and at least a great part of India were covered by water, there lay to the south of the peninsula a vast stretch of continent from Malacca to the shores of Arabia, where now the waves of the Arabian sea are broken only by Ceylon, the Coral islands, the Laccadive, Maldive, and Chagos groups.[1] Professor Owen seems to countenance the same theory when he expresses his belief that Ceylon is the "remnant of a very distinct antecedent group of lands, part of a distinct continent."

On the whole, the Singhalese fauna has more in common with Sumatra, Java, and Borneo, than with India. Roam as you will the jungles or hills of the island from Galle

[1] See *The Ancient World*, by Ansted, p. 322.

to Trincomalee, you will never meet with a tiger, hyena, goat, true leopard, wolf, fox, gazelle, antelope, or vulture.

There is no other country in the world which has, at different periods and by different races, been known under so many names as Ceylon; nor is there any other round which a denser cloud of curious conjecture has gathered. It is mentioned both by Pliny and Strabo. Dionysius Periegetos, the geographer, speaks of it as "the mother of the most stately of elephants." Onesicritus and Megasthenes, companions of Alexander the Great, allude to its richness in gold and pearls. From information derived from the court of Sandracottus, the latter author described the island as very fertile, divided by a river, and as having one part infested with wild beasts, and elephants better suited for war than those of India; the other part producing gold, gems, and pearls. The inhabitants, according to this writer, were called Palæogoni, a word suggestive in the original Greek of the sons of Pali, the colonists who emigrated to Ceylon with Wijayo.

Later writers down to the end of the last

century did not add very much to an exact knowledge of the island. Even the great Marco Polo seems to have been unable to pick up much accurate information about it. He tells us, however, that it was the best island of its size on earth; that its circumference used to be 3600 miles, but in his time was only 2400, the balance having been swept away by a strong north wind (as a matter of fact Ceylon is only 700 miles round). He adds that the king's name was Sendeman, who was independent and ruled over a naked nation of idolaters, with no wheat, but rice and sesamum, of which they made their oil. They lived, he adds, on flesh and milk, and had tree-wine (toddy) and "Brazil wood much the best in the world." He speaks also of the gems, and especially of a ruby belonging to the king, which the emperor of China tried in vain to purchase.

Its names were indeed legion. To the Brahmans it was known, as I have said, as Lanka or Tamba Panni. By the Persians it was called Serendib or Selendib.

The Singhalese get their name from Singhalia (country of lions), a word found also in the varying forms of Sielediba, Serindives, Selin, Syllen,

Sillan, Celan, Zeilan, and Seilan (Marco Polo). Colonel Yule comes to the conclusion that this last word is from the Javanese *sela*, meaning a precious stone. Another of its ancient names was Naga-dipa or snake-island, from the aboriginal worship of the snake, which still lingers in the form of many superstitions connected with that reptile. Taprobane is more familiar to us as a name of Ceylon than are Palasimundæ, Salike (Ptolemy), Simunda, Tenarisim (Moorish = isle of delights), and the Tamul Ilanare. In old Portuguese maps it is put down as Tragana, Trante, Caphane, and Hibenaro. Mediæval geographers called it Siledpa-Camar, Lanka-Camar, Pertina, and Tuphana. It was known to the Chinese as Pa-ou-tchow or isle of gems, and more recently as Sinhala and Seih-lan.[1]

It is impossible at this distance of time, and in the silence of historical records on the point, to decide between the claims of the Chinese and the Burmese as the original inhabitants. A more probable theory brings the islanders from the same stock that colonised the Dekkan, with the various groups of whose languages the Singhalese

[1] For other names see Vincent's *Commerce*, etc., vol. ii. p. 493.

tongue has marked affinity. I cannot, however, say to what extent such a notion harmonises with the Veddah language, as still spoken by the few remaining aborigines.

Passing from conjecture to fact, we know that in the most ancient Indian epic called *Ramayana*, said to be older than the *Iliad*, Ceylon is identified with the scene of a conflict carried on by Rama, king of Oudh, with Rawana, king of Ceylon. And here I may remind my readers that to the student of oriental history the Singhalese records of the past offer far less difficulty than do those of India, a land many of whose ancient annals either lie embedded in graven rock-inscriptions, or are only to be conjectured from the pages of more or less mythical poems. And yet it is not a century since the discovery was made that Ceylon, or, as the Hindoos call it, "the pearl on the brow of India," can boast of continuous written chronicles which are rich in historical facts, and date back in one unbroken record to the fifth century before Christ. From these chronicles the truth stands clearly out that long before the Romans had set foot in Britain, long before the Celtic inhabitants of our own islands had learned the barest rudiments of civilisation, the Singhalese were a powerful nation, not unskilled in some at least of the arts and sciences, and living a life from day to day adorned and made beautiful by the refinements of luxury.

Attracted by the far-famed sanctity of the island, Gautama (Buddha) visited it in order to raise the people from their degraded condition as pagans. This Gautama, or Sakya Muni, who attained to Buddhaship or the state of a divinely perfect being, and was born B.C. 624, was the son of one Suddhodhana, a prince of a small state near Oudh, on the borders of Nepaul, who by heaping every indulgence upon his son tried but in vain to keep him from a life of asceticism.[1] On three separate occasions Gautama visited Ceylon. The first time was commemorated by

[1] It is said that his choice was finally made by his seeing for the first time the body of a dead man, as he was walking along a road with his preceptor; reminding us of the old ballad—

On looking up and looking round,
She saw a dead man on the ground,
And from his nose unto his chin
The worms crawl'd out, the worms crawl'd in.

Then she unto the parson said,
"Shall I be so when I am dead?"
"Oh yes! oh yes!" the parson said,
"You will be so when you are dead."

the erection of a stupendous dagoba at Bintenne, or, as it was then called, Mahayangana, still standing after the lapse of twenty centuries, a huge circular mound of brickwork 360 feet round and 100 feet high. In 1602 a traveller spoke of this dagoba as perfect, and of a dazzling white with a gilded pyramid on the top. The only temple now at Bintenne is a low mean building of whitened mud, covered outside with rude mythological drawings, and standing in the middle of some thirty squalid huts. Once it was surrounded by what is called in the annals "the agreeable Mahanaca garden, the assembly place of the Yakkhos (aboriginals)."

It was on the occasion of Gautama's third visit that he left a souvenir in the shape of the *Sri-pada* or sacred footprint on Adam's Peak. "When the Dewa heard that Buddha was in Ceylon, then called Lanka, he asked him to leave an impression of his foot on the mountain of which he was guardian. In the midst of the assembled Dewas, Buddha, looking towards the east, made the impression of his foot, about 5 feet in length. This impression remained to show that Lanka is the inheritance of Buddha, and that his religion will here flourish." "In a later age," says Tennent, "the hollow in the lofty rock that crowns the summit was said by the Brahmans to be the footstep of Siva, by the Buddhists of Buddha, by the Gnostics of Ieu, by the Mohammedans of Adam, whilst the Portuguese authorities were divided between the conflicting claims of St. Thomas and the eunuch of Candace, Queen of Ethiopia."[1]

From the landing of Wijayo in B.C. 543, on the very day when Gautama Buddha died at the age of eighty under the *sal* tree in Kusinara, we have in the pages of the *Mahawanso*, written in Pali verse, a complete and minute history of the first great dynasty down to the death of Mahasen, the last monarch of his race, who died

[1] The religion of Buddha had been sown and had flourished in an age and a country famous for their literature. As a consequence, its doctrines and discipline were indelibly fixed by means of Sanskrit, one of the most perfect languages in the world, during or immediately after the age of its founder. Again and again furious zealots tried to destroy its records and to extirpate its votaries. But the refugees when driven from India carried their books with them and took refuge in Ceylon, where the sacred writings still exist, either in the original tongue or in one closely allied to it, known to philologists as "high Prakrit," of which a Hindoo writer says that "Sanskrit is spoken by the gods, Prakrit by benevolent genii." These writings are called in Pali *Pitakattayan*, from *pitakan*, a basket, and *tayo*, three. They are in three divisions: 1, *Winaya*, addressed to priests; 2, *Sutra*, addressed to laity; 3, *Abhidharunna*, addressed to Dewas and Brahmas of the celestial worlds. The text was preserved orally till the reign of Walagambahu (B.C. 88), when it was put into writing.

A.D. 301. From the beginning of the fourth century the same record carries on the history of the kings, Suluwanse and others, men "of a lower race," and ends with the year 1758, when the Dutch occupation was drawing to its close. The later portions of the poem are compiled from such native records as were fortunate enough to escape a general destruction of such documents at the hands of an apostate Raja, Singha I., in the sixteenth century. From this and other sources we are able with exact precision to compile an unbroken list of 165 sovereigns, whose reigns covered a period of 2341 years, down to the occupation of the island by the British at the beginning of the present century.

It is not my purpose to give here a detailed account of the various dynasties, wars, and revolutions, in which Singhalese history is so rich, and of which by far the greater part are now of little interest except to the student. I shall confine myself to such a rapid sketch of events as will be enough for the general reader, referring any who desire more details to the list of works placed in the Appendix.

Wijayo, whose landing has been mentioned, was a ne'er-do-weel prince, who was driven by his father from Bengal. On his marriage with a Singhalese princess he obtained supreme power by a wholesale massacre of native chiefs. Five-and-thirty years later, when he lay dying, he sent to his father entreating him to allow his younger brother Panduwasa to succeed him, which he did, Panduwasa on his accession (B.C. 504) taking to wife a cousin of Gautama. From the death of this prince down to the reign of Devenipiatissa (B.C. 306), the native history is for the most part peaceful and uneventful. Many villages and towns were built, timber was planted, tanks, canals, and irrigation works were constructed, and in 437 we first hear of the celebrated Anuradhapoora as the capital city.

It was King Devenipiatissa who sent an embassy in B.C. 306 to King Asoka bearing presents of "eight varieties of pearls, sapphires, lapis-lazuli, rubies, and a right-handed chank-shell (*Turbinella rapa*)." This last was of peculiar value for superstitious reasons, on account of its reversed whorls. In return he received a *chowrie*, or fly-flapper, a diadem, a state sword, a parasol, a pair of gold slippers, a crown, a vase, a howdah, and sundry vessels; to which were added sacred water from the Ganges, some costly aromatic drugs, sandal-wood, and "a virgin of royal birth and great beauty." Devenipiatissa's successor was Tisso I., in whose reign Buddhism was first formally established as the national religion. The king had sent an embassy to Dhammasoko, an Indian potentate, who returned costly gifts, and added ghostly counsel, exhorting the Singhalese to "take refuge in Buddha, his religion and his priesthood." The bearer of this message was Mahindo, the son of Dhammasoko, and a priest of Buddha. On his arrival the new faith was formally set up; multitudes flocked to the preaching of doctrines that were a strange contrast to anything heard before; colleges and temples were built, and to complete the work Mahindo sent his nephew Arittho to bring over his sister Sanghametta to establish a female order. With this lady was brought over a branch of the sacred Bo tree under which Gautama had attained his Buddhaship, and which was planted at Anuradhapoora.

It was in the reign of this same king Tisso I.

that many splendid buildings were erected, among which was the gigantic Thuparamaya. Tisso at his death (B.C. 266) was succeeded by Sura-tisso, who having taken into his service certain Malabar chieftains, Sena and Gutika, was driven by them from power, and shortly afterwards put an end to his own life. The two foreigners ruled well and wisely for thirty years, and were then expelled by the native prince Asela. He in his turn was deposed by the Tamul Elala, who after landing at the Mahawellé river defeated the royal troops at Anuradhapoora. Elala enjoyed a long reign until Gaimono, a nephew of Tisso, rose against him and killed him with his own hand. This Gaimono, who was no unworthy successor of those who had gone before, pushed forward many great works, and brought Anuradhapoora, the royal city, to the height of its splendour.

After the death of Gaimono we may pass over the annals until the first century before Christ, when Walagambahu was driven from his throne by Malabar Tamuls, and remained in exile for fourteen years. An interregnum ensued of anarchy, bloodshed, and disorder, until the restoration of the king, who to celebrate his victory built the huge dagoba at Anuradhapoora, known as the Abhayagiri.

The welfare of the island now received a severe check by the accession of Anula, the daughter-in-law of Walagambahu, a woman who seems to have been a perfect Nero. In B.C. 50 she put her husband, Kuda-tissa, to death in order that she might reign alone, after which she raised several of her lovers to power, only to murder them when she was tired of them; a state of things which went on until her subjects in mad disgust put an end to her. It was not until after many years that Anuradhapoora recovered from the enormities of this shameless ruler.

We get an insight into the condition of Ceylon at this period from the writings of several travellers. Fa Hian, a Chinese, has left us an account of the wealth and power of the sovereign, which agrees closely with what we find in the *Mahawanso* and other native annals. We have also evidence from the western world. St. Ambrose tells us of a Theban who visited the island in the fourth century, and who described the ruler as "the great king who lives in the island of Taprobane." From B.C. 200 to A.D. 500 it was a Golden Age of art and letters in Anuradhapoora, and it is to this period that we must ascribe all the best scientific, historical, and poetical achievements of the Singhalese race.

Passing again over several centuries, the chronicles of which present a monotonous record of recurring war and revolution, and during which as time went on the city of Anuradhapoora began slowly but surely to pass to its decay, we come now to the eighth century after the Christian era, when the royal residence was moved to Pollonaruwa. This was not the only change significant of decline. Incursions from India, constant attacks of marauding Malays, frequent insurrections and civil disorders, all left their mark. For a time indeed, some four centuries later, the ancient glories of Ceylon were revived by Prakrama I., one of her ablest rulers, than whose there is no more illustrious name in the military history of his country. He excelled not only as a soldier but in religious knowledge, grammar, logic, horsemanship, archery, poetry, and music. In his favour Gajabahu, himself an estimable prince, voluntarily abdicated, upon which Prakrama set himself thoroughly to re-establish the prosperity of his kingdom. In his work of reformation he was opposed by the jealousy of Subhala, a tributary and ambitious princess, who after raising the standard of revolt was defeated by the royalist general Rakha, and only saved her own life by absolute submission. No sooner had Prakrama celebrated his triumph at Pollonaruwa than Subhala was again in arms, only to be once more defeated, and this time to meet the death she deserved at the hands of her conqueror.

The rest of the reign of Prakrama was tranquil enough, with the exception of an expedition which he sent under Adikaram into Cambodia, the operations of which resulted in the submission of the whole of Burmah and its annexation to the kingdom of Ceylon. To this we must add the last and greatest of Prakrama's military achievements, which was nothing less than the subjugation of the entire Malabar and Coromandel regions, over which he set up his own son as king. Prakrama died in 1186, and there ensued a long period of anarchy, until his successor Prakrama II. made himself master of the whole island in 1211. Pollonaruwa, which had been the capital for nearly 500 years, was abandoned, and the royal residence moved to Gampola, and subsequently to Kotta and Kandy.

The chief event of the following century was the carrying off of the *Dalada*, or Sacred Tooth of Buddha, by Malabars, in 1303, in whose country it remained for a few years. In 1408 the Chinese Ming Emperor Ching-Tsu sent an expedition to punish an insult offered to some of his subjects at the temple of the Tooth, which carried off King Wijayo-Bahu to China, taking, as some think, the sacred relic also. A few years afterwards the prisoners were restored, and Ceylon was condemned to pay tribute to China, which it did during a period of fifty years.

The name of the island now becomes far more frequent in the writings of travellers who found their way to its shores. Nicolo di Conti, an Italian, says of it in 1501 that it was "a very noble island 3000 miles in circumference, producing gems and cinnamon in great abundance. It was formerly governed by Brahmans, and contains a large lake, in the middle of which stands a city three miles round." A Russian says of it that it is "a port of the Indian sea; antimony, agate, crystal, and *sumbada* (mastick) are found in the vicinity; also elephants and oysters, the former sold by size, the latter by weight." Barboso, a Portuguese, who afterwards sailed with Magellan round the globe, describes Ceylon as "a rich and luxurious land inhabited by Gentiles and ruled by a Gentile king. Both Moors and Gentiles are well-made men nearly white, rather tall and inclined to corpulency. They go bare from the waist, wearing silk and cotton caps on their heads and large earrings. There is a great deal of very good fruit, some not found elsewhere; good elephants are worth 1000 or 1500 ducats."

For many generations before the coming of the Portuguese the history of Ceylon was one of retrogression. Civil strife and external aggression, combined with a growing apathy on the part of the people themselves, were among the principal causes of its decadence. Moors, Malabars, and Malays, each and all in turn were attracted by so rich a prize, and in the course of time gradually reduced it to a mere shadow of its former self.

In 1505 the island may be said to have been rediscovered by the Portuguese under Lorenzo d'Almeida, son of the Governor of Goa, who when on a cruise near the Maldives was driven by the westerly wind into Calambo, changed by the Portuguese to Colombo in honour of the great sailor. The king in his palace at Pollonaruwa heard that "a race of men exceeding white and beautiful" had landed on his shores, "wearing boots and hats of iron and never remaining at rest. They have tubes which make a noise like thunder when it breaks upon Jugandere Parivata, and even louder; and a globe of iron shot from one of them after flying some leagues will break a castle of marble or even of iron."

A friendly welcome was given to the strangers, who promptly erected a pillar to commemorate the conquest (!) of the island and its possession by the king of Portugal: surely one of the coolest pieces of annexation on record, and quite in harmony with the impertinent pretentiousness of Portugal in our own day.

In 1518 the Portuguese, regardless of the

objections of the natives, built a fort at Colombo, thereby drawing upon themselves several furious but unsuccessful attacks. Twenty years later, during a temporary lull in hostilities, a curious ceremony took place at Lisbon, where King John III. solemnly set a crown on the head of an effigy of a Singhalese prince, to whom, under the title of Don Juan, the royal support was henceforth pledged. This Portuguese puppet had troublous times, owing to the restless enmity of Raja Singha, the Lion King, who on one occasion inflicted a heavy defeat upon the Portuguese near Kandy, putting 1700 of them to the sword. Singha seems to have carried all before him until in 1592, at the age of nearly 100 years, he was defeated and killed at the pass of Kadugannawa, now a peaceful roadside station on the rail between Kandy and Colombo. He was a remarkable man, and from first to last a formidable opponent to the invaders of his territory.

The renown of Ceylon, as it reached Europe at the beginning of the seventeenth century, is thus summed up by Purchas in his *Pilgrimage*: "The heavens with their dewes, the ayre with a pleasant holesomenesse and fragrant freshnesse, the waters in their many rivers and fountaines, the earth diversified in aspiring hills, lowly vales, equal and indifferent plaines, filled in her inward chambers with mettals and jewels, in her outward court and upper face stored with whole woods of the best cinnamon that the sunne seeth, besides fruits, oranges, leimans, etc., surmounting those of Spain; fowles and beasts both tame and wild, among which the elephant, honoured by a naturall acknowledgement of excellence of all other elephants in the world, these all have conspired and joined in common league to present unto Zeilan the chiefe of worldly treasures and pleasures with a long and healthful life in the inhabitants to enjoy them, no marvel then if sense and sensualitie have there stumbled on a Paradise."

Now came the dawn of a great change. In 1639 another Singha, being too weak to repeat his ancestor's victories, sent to Batavia entreating the help of the Dutch, who nothing loth came and took possession first of Batticaloa and Trincomalee, and soon afterwards of Negombo and Galle.

For several years now the island was torn from one end to the other by a desultory warfare, ending at last in 1658 by the capture of Colombo, after a long blockade, during which the Portuguese defenders suffered privations culminating in the horrors of cannibalism. Jaffna also fell into Dutch hands, and thus after extending over 153 years the rule of the Portuguese came to an end. It is a fact that has often been remarked upon, that whereas all traces of the later Dutch rule, lasting for 137 years, have in our own day disappeared, those of the Portuguese still remain in many particulars. You can make yourself understood by the use of Indo-Portuguese, at least all along the coast, as well as in some of the inland districts, where Dutch is quite useless. While on the one hand Roman Catholicism disputes with Buddhism the majority of religious professors, on the other the members of the Dutch Reformed Church are but an insignificant handful. It is to be remarked, however, that whereas men of Portuguese extraction are to be found now only in the operative and artisan class, not a few of the Dutch burghers hold appointments in the Government civil service.

The new-comers found it by no means easy to reckon with the irrepressible Singha, who little relished the way in which his new-found allies had reproduced the fable of the monkey and the cakes. But the Dutch steadily gave their thoughts rather to trade than to war, and by turning every possible source of income into a government monopoly, they gave to their new possession the character of a mere trading company's depot, rather than that of a political dependency.

In 1672 a squadron of French ships surprised Trincomalee, which, however, the Dutch speedily recaptured. At the death of Singha II. in 1687, after a long reign, Suria became king, a man who preferred peace to the sword, and did much to restore Buddhism to its old splendour and power. He ruled for twenty-two years, and was followed by his son Kundisala, inclined like his father to peaceful pursuits, but only because he had no taste for anything that checked his own self-gratification. Cruel, unprincipled, and headstrong, Kundisala was as bad a prince as ever held sway in Ceylon. He carried matters to such a pitch that his nobles rebelled and provoked the interference of the Dutch.

At this period not a few of the governors sent out from the Hague seem to have been men of very unworthy ambitions. One named Vuyst carried his arrogant extortions so far that he was put on his trial at Batavia and executed. His successor Versluys, who was recalled in 1732, was little better, and heaped every kind of oppression on the Singhalese, especially in the matter of the rice monopoly. On the other hand, such names as Falck and Van Goens are those of men of a very different stamp, under whom Ceylon flourished and its commerce largely increased.

We have now reached in this brief sketch the period of British rule. In 1782, when England was at war with Holland, Lord Macartney, Governor of Madras, sent a fleet to attack the Dutch possessions, at the same time despatching an envoy to the native court at Kandy. Trincomalee was taken, but in the temporary absence of the naval force shortly afterwards fell into the hands of the French.

For twelve years we hear no more of the English in Ceylon. But in 1795 General Stewart retook Trincomalee after a three weeks' siege, and then marched to Jaffna, which surrendered without a blow. In the next spring Negombo followed suit, as did Colombo and Galle. Thus the whole of the maritime districts became annexed to the English Government at Madras almost without resistance from the Dutch, who were at this time in an utterly disorganised state. We hear no more of them as masters of Ceylon. On the whole their occupation was an inglorious one, and their commercial rapacity was responsible for even more baneful results than the bigoted despotism of the Portuguese. The Dutch showed themselves stolid, avaricious, and independent; the Portuguese mercurial, accommodating, and proselytising.

The Kandyan Raja Dhi gave no cordial welcome to the English. At his death in 1798 the Adigar, or prime minister, opened negotiations with Mr. North the governor, which, however, as they were found to involve the murder of a harmless prince, came to nothing. The end of the long line of native kings was now at hand. In 1801 the island was formed into a separate colony, soon after which a wasting war broke out in the hill country; General Macdowall from Colombo and Colonel Barbut from Trincomalee advanced upon Kandy, where they proclaimed as king Muta Samy, brother of the late queen. In the belief that order was restored, the troops returned to Colombo, leaving Major Davie in Kandy with 1500 men. Talawe, the late Adigar, who was an adept at throwing dust in the eyes of the English, appeared suddenly before Kandy, and ordered Major Davie to retire to Trincomalee. The English commander weakly obeyed, and started on his perilous march, reaching the Mahawellé only to find it swollen and impassable. On flank and rear the Kandyans were pressing in formidable numbers ; retreat and advance seemed alike impossible, the only hope of escape lying in a bold attack upon the enemy. Unfortunately Major Davie was not a man equal to the position. He accepted the offer of the wily Adigar to see him and his troops safely across the river, in return for the delivery up of the unfortunate Muta Samy, who was at once impaled before British eyes. Seeing that they had a coward to deal with, the rebels became bolder, and even had the audacity to order Major Davie to disarm his troops and lead them back to Kandy. In vain did his officers expostulate. The first part of the order was carried out, and every Englishman, except three officers, was then led into a rocky defile and massacred. We may be thankful that there are few such pages in English history, and still fewer British officers against whom a charge of cowardly folly can be so fully sustained. Major Davie, execrated by his countrymen, sought a home among the natives, and ended his life many years after in the north of the island.

After this dark episode a desultory war went on for several years, during which Talawe met with his death. In 1815 King Wikrama was taken prisoner by General Brownrigg and sent to Vellore in India, where he died twenty years afterwards. He was the last king of Ceylon, he and his race being for ever excluded from the throne. For some years disorder reigned supreme, the Kandyan nobles submitting to obliteration with an ill grace, but ever weakening their own cause by innumerable dissensions among themselves. Wide districts were laid waste, villages burnt, crops destroyed, many lives lost. There is no knowing how long such a state of things might have lasted but for a sudden stroke of fortune. This was nothing less than the capture by the British of the celebrated

Dalada, or Tooth of Buddha. Directly the Singhalese learnt that the relic was in white hands, they offered no further resistance; and from that time to this the sword has never been drawn in Ceylon.

It is no part of my purpose to sketch the later political history of the island. It is enough to say that from time to time Ceylon has been fortunate in having English governors of ability, in not a few instances men exceptionally able and willing to open up her wonderful resources. There have been dark as well as bright spots in the records of the last seventy years, but on the whole peace, plenty, and prosperity have steadily added to the lustre of a colony which is one of the brightest gems in the crown of Great Britain.

The Governor of Ceylon receives a salary of 80,000 rupees a year. The following is a list down to the present time:—

Governor of Madras	1796	Sir E. Barnes . . .	1820
Hon. F. North . .	1798	Sir E. Paget . . .	1823
Sir J. Maitland . .	1805	Sir E. Barnes . . .	1824
General Wilson . .	1811	Sir W. Horton . .	1831
Sir R. Brownrigg .	1812	Rt. Hon. S. Mackenzie	1837

SIR COLIN CAMPBELL .	1841	RT. HON. W. GREGORY	1871
LORD TORRINGTON .	1847	A. N. BIRCH, ESQ. . .	1875
SIR G. ANDERSON . .	1850	SIR J. R. LONGDEN .	1877
SIR H. G. WARD . .	1855	SIR J. DOUGLAS . .	1883
SIR C. T. MACCARTHY	1860	HON. SIR A. GORDON .	1883
SIR H. G. ROBINSON .	1865	SIR A. E. HAVELOCK .	1890

NOTE.—On the marriage of the Infanta of Portugal with Charles II. in 1662 England acquired Bombay as a portion of the bride's dowry. The fourteenth article of the treaty drawn up on the occasion provided that "if the island of Zeilon should by any means be recovered by Portugal, the king shall be bound to deliver the port of Galle to England, and the cinnamon trade be divided between them." Owing to the course of events this provision remained a dead letter.

CHAPTER III

THE PEOPLE

THE total number of the inhabitants of Ceylon in the year 1881 was 2,763,984, to which (according to the Colonial Office list) must be added about 30,000 of mixed races inhabiting the Maldive archipelago, 500 miles to the west, speaking a language akin to old Singhalese. Of this number the Singhalese proper, chiefly in the south and south-west of the island, numbered 1,846,614, descendants probably of men who came originally from the banks of the Ganges, and conquered the aboriginal Veddahs, who now to the number of a few thousands live a nomadic and semi-savage life in the interior.[1]

In course of time, as stated in the preceding chapter, the Singhalese were in their turn driven out of the northern districts by Tamuls from the

[1] Note C.

Malabar coast of India. These Tamuls at the present time number about 700,000, rather less than a third of the whole population, and are no less distinct in race and language than in their religion, which is that of Siva.

Both the Singhalese as Buddhists and the Tamuls as Brahmans are in theory, and possibly in practice, at least equal if not superior to average Christians. The Buddhist believes in metempsychosis, or transmigration of souls, and that as a man acts in this life so will be his future lot. He believes also that the purified spirits of the virtuous attain after successive embodiments to the state of Nirvana, a dreamlike passive existence of unalloyed contemplation. The three fundamental aphorisms of Buddha are: 1, refrain from evil; 2, practise virtue; 3, restrain the heart.[1]

Numerically, the Singhalese form one of the smallest races on the earth; their language, which belongs to the Indo-European group, is perhaps more beautiful in sound than any other, being softer and more musical than the purest Italian. They are described by Marco Polo, and also by

[1] Note D.

an earlier traveller in the fourth century, Ludovico Barthelema, as not only unwarlike folk, but as actually cowardly in fight. This is an estimate which, with the pages of their history open before us, it is difficult to agree with. I believe that if the warriors of Lanka had possessed a Macaulay or a Prescott to record their deeds of prowess, there are places among its mountain fastnesses which would have been handed down as magic names vying even with Marathon and Thermopylæ. Nor must it be forgotten that, while the nations of Europe have been again and again broken into fragments and reconstructed under many different forms, all more or less heterogeneous, Ceylon has retained her almost primeval identity, and can point to her language, her religion, and her sacred monuments, as triumphant evidence of the fact. It is a matter that has not been sufficiently investigated, how it comes about that the Buddhist nations of the earth have preserved their individuality for a longer period than any other people, excepting only the nomadic tribes.

As a Brahman, the Tamul does not worship Brahma nor dedicate temples to him, but believes in him merely as a self-existent Intelligence. The history of Brahma is in many respects a reproduction of that of Abraham, to whose name his bears a close resemblance, as does also that of his wife Sarasvadi to Sara.

Next to these come the Moormen, numbering 184,000, sprung from Mohammedans who more than twenty centuries ago first found their way to Ceylon. For 1500 years they held the trade of the island in their hands, and at the present time are still among the shrewdest men of business in Colombo.

Then come swarms of Asiatic and African immigrants, Malays, Javanese, Parsees, Afghans, Negroes, and Kafirs, as well as a large mixed multitude who belong to no one race. Finally, there are about 5000 Europeans and some 18,000 Eurasian burghers, or half-caste Portuguese and Dutch, making what is now probably a total population of 3,000,000.

The Singhalese are slightly formed, many of the men being of quite feminine proportions. Their skin is of a cinnamon colour, and their faces are more like Europeans than most other Asiatics, with black or hazel eyes. They have often wonderful heads of hair, which they draw back with a hoop and fasten up in a *cundy* or knot, adorned with a good-sized tortoise-shell comb. Some of them wear petticoats, and others a *comboy*, or cloth three yards long, in which they swathe their loins. In the Kandyan district the upper classes attach much importance to a respectable rotundity of person, which they acquire by wrapping their bodies in many folds of white linen. Singhalese hands and feet are small and delicate, and many of the men allow the little finger nail to grow to a preposterous length—a practice common also among Chinamen and Tahitians, who wish it to be understood that they never soil their hands with manual labour, for the Singhalese never work when they can avoid it.

The Tamuls are chiefly employed as coolies in the country districts, where when at work they wear nothing but a small square kerchief called *amudé*. In the town they are distinguished by their turbans and earrings, as well as by their stronger and more manly frames and graver countenances, of a dark coffee colour. Their looks do not belie them, for they are sober, active, and far more industrious than the Singhalese, and do all kinds of heavy work, as road-makers, porters, and labourers.

Here is a description of an ideal Singhalese belle as given by a native connoisseur: "Her hair should be abundant as the tail of a peacock, long as a palm leaf of ten moons' growth; her eyebrows arched like the rainbow; her eyes long as the almond and dark as midnight when there is no moon. Her nose should be slender like the bill of the hawk; her lips full and red like coral or the young leaf of the iron-tree; her teeth small and closely set, and like jessamine buds or a pearl when taken from the shell; her neck should be thick and round like the stem of a plantain; her chest wide, her bosom full in form like a young coco-nut her waist small, to be clasped almost within two outspread hands; her hips should be round and her limbs tapering; the soles of her feet without any arch or hollow; the surface of her body soft, delicate, smooth, and rounded, no bones, sinews, or angles visible; not a blemish on her skin, the tint of which should be bright and brown."

As a people the Singhalese are courteous and even ceremonious, invariably treating one another with deference. There is no arrogance among the upper classes nor servility among the lower; the one is affably condescending, the other respectful and modest. They are not convivial but exceedingly sociable, tremendous gossips, and not over *galant*; indeed the more refined sentiments of chivalry do not seem to thrive in tropical countries. There are few large villages. The Singhalese appear to share the instinct of all agricultural folk which leads them to congregate in small numbers, or to inhabit detached dwellings each standing in its own little plot. For the most part they build their huts in low sheltered situations, out of the way of the wind, and near their padi fields. Outside the door they have ready at hand all they need: rice, their staff of life; milk from cows and buffaloes; fruit and oil. From the travelling pedlar they get by barter a few comforts now and then: a little salt, or tobacco, or dry fish, or a gay handkerchief. The men do all the heavy field-work, the women the weeding, reaping, milking, spinning, and looking after the domestic economies. The richer people spend much time in calling upon one another and discussing their neighbours, listening to stories or musical performances, and playing games of cards taught them by the Portuguese. The ladies are very fond of a game something like back-gammon.

There is not much to look at in the interior of a native hut. A couch or two, a few stools and mats, two or three ware dishes, a few miscellaneous vessels and baskets, with a wooden rice mortar and pestle. In the corner stands a stone handmill for the *korrakan* and other small grain, looking much like a Celtic *querne*. The inventory is completed by a coco-nut scraper, a circular iron rasp in a wooden stand, used for mincing the nut for curry. They rise with the sun, and go to bed at 9 P.M. on a mat near a bit of fire. At noon they have their principal meal of rice and curry, to which those who can afford it add eggs, fowls, game, etc. An hour before bedtime they have their evening meal, very often a mess with coagulated milk; cheese they have never tasted, and butter only in the form of the clarified mess called *ghee*.

The girls almost invariably marry very young, and an old maid is quite a *rara avis*.

CHAPTER IV

COLOMBO, PEREDENIYA, KANDY, AND NUWARA ELIYA

THE moment we appear at the door of the hotel in Colombo a crowd of jinrikishas comes up at full speed clamouring for patronage. Let us take one and see all we can in the course of a morning drive through the city.

Making first for the native quarter of Pettah, or Black-town, we pass picturesque Slave island, which gets its name from the following incident. One night, in the old slave times before the year 1844, the Kafir slaves in a certain house in the Fort, in consequence of cruel treatment, rose and murdered a whole family. Thenceforward the slaves were every evening put into punts at sunset, and rowed to what was then an island, where they were kept under safe guard until the morning.

Here, too, is a lovely lagoon of considerable

extent, bordered by charming gardens and groves of palms. One of the delights of Colombo life is an evening sail on the bosom of this lake. A little farther on and we are in crowded Pettah, stretching away down to the harbour, which it skirts for a mile or two until it is stopped by the Kalani Ganga, the river which originally gave to Colombo its name of Kalanbua or Kalambu, afterwards, as I have already said, changed by the Portuguese to its present form in honour of the great navigator.

A drive through Pettah for the first time is a veritable revelation to an Englishman. The swarming crowds are made up, like the multitude on the day of Pentecost, of Parthians, Medes, Elamites, and the rest. Men in fezzes, men in hats, men in turbans, men in petticoats, men in trousers, men in boots, men in great peaked red or yellow slippers, men in nothing at all but the burnished livery of the sun. Few places on earth can show a more varied mingling of the human race, the majority of whom are collected in groups, with apparently nothing to do but catch fleas and gossip idly with their neighbours. Others with a singular quiet gentleness carry on their avocations in the market or the queer little *caddies* or shops. In the length of half a street we meet Singhalese, Kandyans, Tamuls, Arabs, Malays, half-castes, and many others that baffle identification. Yonder comes a *Samanero*, or candidate for the higher grade of the Buddhist priesthood, begging alms in a large brass bowl. Not far off stalks a clean-shaven cleric in bright saffron-coloured robe, under an umbrella carried by an *Abittaya* or boy in white. Here, too, is a Mohammedan *padre* in a green silk gown, with trousers as wide as sacks; and possibly we may meet a veiled Veddah, one of the aboriginal race, now fast disappearing, and rarely to be seen in the towns. Among the crowd is here and there a tall and stalwart Moorman, with yellow-brown Semitic features and black hair crowning a bearded face, dressed in white *caftan* and drawers and wearing a high yellow turban.

One of the first things that strike us is that nine out of ten of the population have been violently spitting blood. But we soon find out that the gory stains on lips and teeth are the result of the universal habit of chewing betel. Every one carries a minute bag (*hembili*) either in his turban or in the *sarong*, a strip of red woollen stuff worn round the loins. If we open one of these bags we shall find some areca nut, betel leaves (four a penny and with a pungent peppery taste), tobacco (which grows on the alluvial lands at the river mouths), ginger, a pair of tiny scissors, and a small box of *chunam*, or fine lime made from calcined pearl shells. A pinch of the *chunam* as big as a pea, a morsel of areca, with one of ginger, added to an atom of tobacco, forms the dainty morsel; all is wrapped up together in a betel leaf and chewed for hours; a brilliant red dye flowing from the areca, which is more of a stimulant than a narcotic. Many of the natives suffer from cancer in the cheek from this habit of chewing caustic lime.[1]

As we pass along our ears are sure to be tortured by the strident creaking of the bullock *bhandies* (Tamul, *wandi*) with their covering of plaited coco-leaves, drawn by mild-eyed humped zebus. Few horses are seen, and an ass never; dogs looking more than half jackals abound, as do shoals of lively little black pigs and melancholy fowls, with here and there a leggy goat. As we

[1] Note E.

turn into the market-place we barely escape collision with a little carriage that rushes headlong by, drawn by a pair of brisk Burmese "tats" driven by a dark Tamul in white jacket and red turban. There are any number of these carriages to be hired in the town. Should you prefer to be your own "whip," the horse-boy will run alongside the whole distance, now and then jumping up on to the step to take a rest.

This Pettah market is the Covent Garden of Colombo, where lie for sale many things curious to a stranger's eye. Pine-apples a foot long for a penny, coco-nuts by the thousand, bananas, yams, breadfruit, and jaks, weighing from five to fifty pounds each. Here are custard-apples, scaly and rather disappointing; mangoes, kidney-shaped, with a tough green skin and yellow fibrous flesh, smelling slightly of turpentine, lying round a large oblong stone. Close by are shaddocks or poncolos, a cross between orange and lemon, finer here than in the West Indies; poor apples and indifferent oranges, green, dry and stringy; limes, rose-apples, guavas, figs, granadillas, passion-fruit, papayas, and mangostans, which when just picked are as cold as iced water, and taste like perfumed snow. Yonder on a board lies a huge turtle, which is being cut up piecemeal while alive; it is on its back, with breast, lungs, and viscera all bare. A Buddhist will not actually take life, for is he not bound by the obligation *Panatipataweramanisikkhapadangsamadiyami*, which being interpreted means, "I will observe the precept that forbids the taking of life"? But he does what is far worse in the torturing of a creature like this, because he fancies the slices will have a better flavour; just as with the same indifference to suffering he carries his pig home hanging from a pole passed between its fore and hind legs.

The life and labours of the people are for the most part carried on in full view of the outer world; there are no doors or shutters to screen the stuffy-looking interiors. Details of the toilet, usually associated in Europe with a certain privacy, seem here to be singled out specially for performance in public. With unembarrassed *sang froid* (if such an expression can be allowed with the thermometer at 100°) the native male or female goes through various tasks of a strictly personal nature under a blaze of publicity. Here is a bronzed artist's model sitting demurely at his door brushing his teeth with a bit of split wood. Hard by is a bathing place, where *douche* and shower are indulged in regardless of criticism by the bystanders, who are probably too busily engaged in their own entomological pursuits to give a thought to their neighbour's ablution. When night comes, or the wet monsoon is blowing, a screen of matting or a lateen shutter is drawn across the entrance of the houses; but in this bright burning sunshine one can discern the most private episodes of family life.

Leaving the native quarter, of which a rapid glance can give no adequate idea, we direct our human steeds now to a tour round the more fashionable parts of Colpetty and the Cinnamon gardens, where we may drive by the hour together along beautiful level red roads shaded everywhere by a wealth of blossoming trees, and lined by innumerable varieties of shrubs and flowers. Here let me mention that the made roads throughout Ceylon are invariably of splendid construction, equalling if they do not surpass the finest Swiss or Norwegian ones. Every native man between the ages of eighteen and fifty-five is bound to do six days' work a year on them, unless he commutes the labour by a payment of one and a half rupee in the country or two rupees in the town.

Out along the Kalani road, upon which a few miles out of Colombo stands a large Buddhist temple with a good library, we pass along under arcades of feathery bamboo, past groups of low brown huts dotted down amid the most luxuriant masses of foliage. Around each dwelling-place is a little patch of korrakan (a small grain), Indian corn, millet, or pumpkins, garnished with rows of onions, garlic, red-pepper, curry seeds, and sweet potatoes; the whole forming a glorious contrast with the brown huts and the bright red soil strongly impregnated with oxide of iron. The scene is one in which nature seems to run riot. It is like a lovely wild garden; everywhere

Droops the heavy-blossom'd bower, hangs the heavy-fruited tree.

It is most lovely when seen in the cool light of early morning, as the sun strikes level through the trees, throwing long shadows from the palms and breaking into a thousand arrowy flecks of gold. Or in the evening it is scarcely less entrancing when the sinking lord of day is firing the west with ruddy shafts, and flooding the cloud-world with hues that defy the palette of the painter.

The best way to get a glimpse of the mountain scenery is to take the train from Colombo to Kandy, a four hours' trip. The line is a fine piece of engineering 74½ miles long, some parts of which cost £27,000 a mile. The gauge is Indian, 5 feet 6 inches, and in some places the gradient is as much as 1 in 45.

For two hours after leaving the Maradana terminus the rail runs through level marshy jungle, with padi fields and water meadows, in which herds of black buffalo stand in the shade, or more often lie half-hidden in water, while the pretty white "cattle-keeper herons" (*Ardea bubulcus*) pick the insects from off their backs. After passing Rambukana the line begins to climb, passing for an hour or more through scenery finer than that of any other railway I know. With many zigzags the train winds up the steep northern face of a vast amphitheatre of hills. Luxuriant masses of dense forest fill the ravines, lovely creepers fling themselves from tree to tree in mid-air, while here and there falls a cascade like a gossamer veil down the huge blocks of gneiss. The whole face of the far-reaching valley is one vast park, edged by the lofty blue range of mountains that calmly and proudly keep their watch beyond its southern margin. By and by the line passes "Sensation Rock," whence in old times the Kandyan kings used to hurl their prisoners of war,—a wonderful point of view under overhanging crags so close to the edge of a vertical precipice that you could toss a lime 1800 feet sheer down out of the window. Far below the green countryside lies bathed in sleepy sunshine, with scattered huts and gaudy gardens and terraced fields.[1]

Another fifteen minutes and we are at Peredeniya, where in the year 1371 the king Wikrama Bahu kept his court, but now famous for its most beautiful botanic gardens, 150 acres in extent; to reach which we cross a very fine bridge over the Mahawellé Ganga, built of satin wood on the American wedge principle,

[1] Here are some of the pretty musical names of places between Colombo and the hills: *Kelaniya, Mirigama, Kaduagomua, Kaduganawa, Talawakeli, Nanuoya* (the vowels pronounced as in Italian).

with one single span of 800 feet. Reaching the gardens we pass down an avenue of superb india-rubber trees (*Ficus elastica*), which are grown in England in little pots and kept in sitting-rooms for the sake of their pretty bright leaves. Here they are noble forest trees spreading 40 or 50 feet on every side, while, like some other Ceylon trees, the trunks at their base throw out a circle of roots often 100 or 200 feet in diameter. These extraordinary roots look like huge snakes, whence they get their native name meaning "snake-tree." As often as not these roots grow up again from the earth, and form an army of stout props for the protection of the parent tree.

As we reach the end of the avenue we find ourselves in front of a grand clump of every kind of palm, foreign as well as indigenous, each wreathed with flowery creepers and fantastic vegetable parasites. Among them are strangers from China, Australia, India, the West Indies, and New Guinea, as well as thorny climbing palms, or *rattans*, from the archipelago, with stems a finger thick and 200 or 300 feet long. On the left a path leads to the director's bungalow, embedded in climbing plants, with orchids, begonias, ipomœas, bromelias, white asclepias, petunias, fuschias, and a hundred other flowers, combining to fashion a happy hunting-ground for numbers of butterflies, squirrels, lizards, and birds. From this bungalow (on the verandah of which I well remember that I first made acquaintance with the delicious passion-fruit) a broad velvety lawn slopes down to a belt of tall trees, beyond which are the Mahawellé and a range of hills crowned with verdure.

Next we find our way past giant bamboos 2 feet thick and 100 high to the marvellous fernery, on the bank of a cool piece of water gay with lotus and red bindweed, a very dream of paradise. Here are ferns, from the tiny species like a delicate moss to the *Alsophila* tree-fern 30 feet high, with deep cut fronds 12 feet in length. Farther on is a curiosity greater although less beautiful, in the shape of a very old fig-tree with a great roof of boughs supported by a host of pillar props. When I saw it, it was quite bare of leaves, and its naked branches looked as if they were covered with large hanging brown fruit, like old leathern bags. We clapped our hands and all the fruit flew away, being in reality nothing but a multitude of flying foxes, which took to flight with shrill screams.

A walk of 3½ miles through a continuous suburb, along a road lined the whole way with houses in little gardens of breadfruit and pepper trees, brings us to Kandy, called by the natives *Maha-nuwara*, the railway station of which is 1602 feet above sea-level. Here the Governor has a country house built of *chunam* or burnt lime, which takes a high polish and looks not unlike alabaster. The real objects of interest in the old Kandyan capital are the Palace and the Buddhist Temple. The former was built in 1600 by Portuguese prisoners, on which account no doubt certain portions of it have a European appearance. It must once have been an extensive building, although according to our ideas not imposing. The rooms at present in use have been altered, the spacious audience hall being now used as a district court-house, in which are some columns of teak with elaborately carved capitals. Here the kings used to be approached by their ministers on all-fours, with their faces close to the earth and literally licking the dust. The façade of the palace is a fine one, with a moat in front now filled up; it stands on the edge of a wide open space where formerly elephant fights were held, and beyond which stretches an artificial tank three-quarters of a mile long, in which is visible, on a little island, what was once a harem, and is still made use of for the storage of explosives in the shape of gunpowder. On the farther side rise the hills which encircle the city. The situation of Kandy is very lovely, but the place possesses little beyond a historical interest. Surely good Bishop Heber, who here wrote "From Greenland's icy mountains," must have had a touch of "liver" when he spoke of it as a place "where every prospect pleases and only man is vile." So far from being vile in any sense, the average Tamul or Singhalese is by no means inferior in morality to numbers of Englishmen who are seen every Sunday in church or chapel.

Hard by the palace stands the world-renowned temple of the Sacred Tooth, the Maligawa Dalada, which is to the Buddhist what Mecca and the Kaaba are to the Mohammedan. Looked at from the outside it is not an attractive edifice.

On entering we pass through one or two gloomy chambers until we come to a solid silver door, the frame of which is inlaid with ivory, opening into a small and ill-lighted recess called the *Wihara*,[1] containing a massive table of silver, behind which is the *Carandua*, or shrine of the same metal, 5 feet high and shaped like a half-egg or *dagoba*. Within are five other shrines one inside the other, of which two are literally alive with precious stones and festooned with jewelled chains, the smallest containing the Tooth, the palladium of Ceylon, resting upon a golden lotus leaf and hidden from the eyes of the world. It is never seen except for a few seconds once a year, when a priest places it in a loop of gold wire and holds it up for the adoration of the assembled worshippers. The original relic (for alas! the present one is neither human nor venerable) had an eventful and a chequered history. The Brahman Pandu, lord paramount of India, some centuries before the Christian era, heard that his vassal Guhasiwa worshipped a piece of bone, this being nothing else than the left canine tooth of Gautama

[1] A *Wihara* means properly a monastery or temple in which priests reside.

Buddha, which for eight centuries was preserved in Kalinga, the modern Jaganath. Pandu in great wrath sent and carried off the relic and sought to destroy it. This he found difficulty in accomplishing. When the tooth was put into a pan of burning charcoal a lotus rose from out of the flames, with the tooth unharmed on the surface. When struck with a heavy hammer it received no damage; tossed into a filthy sewer, a lovely garden of flowers sprang up round it. The natural result of these portents was that Pandu was converted to Buddhism and restored the tooth. In A.D. 302, when it was threatened with danger, a daughter of Kriti-sri-megha-wama concealed it in the tresses of her hair and fled with it to Ceylon, where it remained for 900 years, until it came into the hands of the Tamuls, being a few years afterwards recovered by Prakrama II. In 1560 the Portuguese Constantini de Braganza seized it and carried it to Goa, where, according to the unimpeachable witness of Captain J. Ribeiro, it was solemnly pounded to atoms by the archbishop, in the presence of the viceroy and his court. The present tooth is 2 inches long and 1 inch thick at the base, and most certainly never could have belonged to a human being.

A scarcely less venerated and probably far more genuine relic is the *Patra*, or alms-pot of Buddha, also preserved in this temple. It is the Holy Grail of Buddhism, with the same mystical powers of nourishment as are ascribed to the Grail in European legends. German writers have indeed traced in the romances of the Grail remarkable indications of an oriental origin, emanating possibly from this very alms-pot of Buddha at Kandy.

In the first week of the new year I was present in the temple of the Dalada at a festival service. Great crowds assembled, every worshipper bringing an offering of champac or some other sweet-smelling flower. Musicians made discordant music with tam-tams (Singhalese, *tamme-tam*),[1] pipes, flutes, cymbals, and chank-shells.[2] Priests in the saffron robes of their order chanted lugubriously in monotonous cadence; the air was hot and heavy with sickening fumes of incense, and the temple chambers were ablaze with many lights.

[1] The *tamme-tam* is a kind of kettle covered with a skin and beaten with a *kadi-pow*.

[2] *Chanquo* is the native word for pearl oyster, connected with *concha*.

The most impressive part of the function to me was the recollection that I was taking part in the cultus of a Being to whom 350,000,000 of my fellow-men, or one-fourth of the whole population of the earth, owe religious obedience.[1]

Apart from their office the priests, who number one in 400 of the people, do not—so far as I have observed—either merit or enjoy much respect from the laity. They are almost invariably illiterate and in no way superior to the masses around them. While as members of a mendicant order they outwardly possess but a few articles of small value, they are in reality among the richest persons in Ceylon. There are very extensive lands belonging to many of the temples, grants made by former kings, and reaching back in some instances to the time of Christ.

The priests are of two grades: 1, *Samanero* (from *sramana,* ascetic) or *Ganinnanso* (from *gana,* an association); and 2, *Terunnanse* (from Pali *thero,* an elder). They are commonly known by their Chinese name of *bonze,* meaning "one entitled to reverence." They wear yellow robes folded back on the left shoulder, leaving the right breast bare.

[1] Note F.

Celibacy and abstinence from flesh-meat are compulsory, the latter obligation sitting more lightly now than in former days ; their principal food is rice and eggs, which they are bound to receive only as alms and to consume before noon, the later hours being *wikala* or forbidden. They are supposed to live wholly upon the voluntary charity of the people, being prohibited from asking for anything. It is stated in an inscription of the twelfth century at Pollonaruwa, that it was the king's custom to give to the priests annually five times his own weight in alms. Their daily work is to cleanse the temple, tend the ever-burning lamp, look after the floral offerings, and collect their own food. That they are an ignorant class will not surprise us, when we know that the examination necessary in the case of a *samanero* upon entering (at the age of twenty) the higher grade, has reference solely to his possession of eight material requisites, without which no one is considered eligible. These are: 1, three sets of robes called *sangha-tiya*, *uttarasangaya*, and *antarawasakaya* ; 2, a wooden platter ; 3, an alms-bowl ; 4, a walking-staff ; 5, a sack ; 6, a fan (wherewith to keep his eyes from beholding vanity when he walks abroad); 7, a needle; and 8, a razor. With the last article he is bound to shave his head once a fortnight. That the bald heads get no harm from the fierce heat of the sun might seem astonishing did we not know, as indeed Herodotus long ago has informed us, that exposure tends greatly to make the skull callous.

There is a fine drive at Kandy along a well-made road known as Lady Horton's Walk, which winds among the mountains. On the east side it skirts the deep precipitous valley of Doombera, and affords a splendid view of the roaring Mahawellé Ganga, with the surrounding hills clothed with the tall strongly-smelling lemon-grass (*Andropogon schœnanthus*).

Another hour in the train up past Kandy brings us to Nanuoya, the terminus of the line; whence an uphill walk of four miles along a splendid road leads to Nuwara Eliya, or royal plains, the sanatorium of Ceylon, with a climate at a mean of 57°, that must be to a Tamul like that of Nova Zembla to an Englishman.

Nuwara Eliya (pronounced Nuralia) owes its reputation in great measure to the energy of Sir

Samuel Baker, the well-known traveller, who lived here for eight years. Unfortunately the progress of this place has not answered the expectations of its early friends; in explanation of which various causes are assigned by the knowing ones, into which it is not necessary here to enter. The climate at such an elevation (6200 feet) is such that whereas you leave Colombo at 8 A.M. in sweltering heat, you are glad on reaching Nuwara Eliya in the afternoon to sit near a fire and to order an extra blanket on your bed. At the beginning of the south-west monsoon—that is, from the middle of June to the middle of July—the weather up here is invariably bad, after which it continues more or less unsettled right on to December. There are frequent showers of rain, never, however, of a tropical character, but resembling rather a Scottish mist. The total fall rarely reaches a quarter of that on the lower lands.

Nuwara Eliya consists of little more than a handful of low stone houses scattered about a plateau some three miles long, divided by a stream, and overlooked by Pedrutallagalla (8280 feet), twice as high as Ben Nevis, and the loftiest mountain in Ceylon. The name means "mat-cloth mountain," from the quantities of so-called mat-grass growing at the base. Close at hand are Totapella (8000 feet), Kirigallapotta (7900 feet), and Adam's Peak or Samanella (7700 feet). None of these mountains look as imposing as do many elsewhere of less elevation, in consequence of their rising not from a level base but from highlands.

There is a rest-house at Nuwara Eliya where you may pay sixpence for an egg, two shillings for a pound of very inferior butter, and the same for a bottle of execrable beer. There is also a pretty church with a graveyard stocked with British flowers, and alas! with British bodies as well, for here, although the

Mountains boast of northern health,
Where Europe amid Asia smiles,

Death claims his victims as he does elsewhere.

CHAPTER V

ANURADHAPOORA

FEW persons, even among those who are acquainted with eastern lands, are aware that the above array of soft sounds represents the name of one of the most ancient and remarkable cities in the world, built at a time when in London there was not one stone upon another. In its present ruinous condition Anuradhapoora may be truly called the Palmyra of Ceylon. In the days of its glory, when within the walls of its vast palace of brass ninety kings reigned in succession, the royal city was 52 miles in circumference, or, in other words, 16 miles across in a straight line from the north to the south gate.

Anuradhapoora, called by Ptolemy Anurogrammum, gets its name from a certain prince, Anuradha,[1] who with five companions crossed

[1] The final syllables are from the Sanskrit *grâma*, meaning a city or village.

from India to Ceylon in the year B.C. 500, and founded the city. For twelve centuries it has lain desolate, having been partially destroyed by the Tamuls and deserted at a period when it had already lost much of its pristine glory.

I had often heard of this little-known wonder of the world, and when I found myself within reasonable distance I determined to visit it. It is situated 90 miles almost due north of Kandy, and is known to comparatively few travellers in consequence of its being difficult of access. My friends in the island made me fully aware beforehand of the discomforts I should have to encounter, and I must confess that my experience certainly in no way fell short of their warnings.

Leaving the hill country, we made a short stage the first day to Matale, and then pushed on next morning to Damboola, a considerable village. Near here are the famous cave temples, which lay too far from my route for me to visit. They are of large size and remarkable for the perfect condition of their decorations. They are four in number, situated in a vast natural cavern, and containing forty-eight statues of Buddha. Their formation is due to King Walagambahu, who lived in the first century before Christ. The principal temple is 178 feet long, 80 feet wide, and 25 feet high, with walls and roof painted in colours still brilliant, setting forth various events in the earthly life of the sage.

The next afternoon we reached the tank of Kalawera, a truly stupendous work made in the fifth century, and now just restored by the English Government; it covers 7 square miles with a depth of 20 feet. Some of these ancient tanks equal if they do not surpass the most colossal works in the western world. There are in Ceylon at least thirty of enormous size, with 700 smaller ones. In the twelfth century Prakrama Bahu constructed no less than 1470 of them, which were known as "the seas of Prakrama."

Close by is Vigitapoora, a city which five centuries before the Christian era, when Anuradhapoora itself was but a village, was the fortified residence of a king.

After leaving Vigitapoora our way lay through the Nuwara Kelawa jungle, now depopulated, but once thickly peopled and admirably irrigated. For many miles we passed through dense *chenar* or thorny jungle, with tall *mana* grass growing amid almost impenetrable thickets, and a network of bush and brake and matted stems; thorny shrubs, spiny creepers, and innumerable prickly parasites caught our clothes and scratched our flesh at every step. Now and then the sultry silence was broken by the distant bark of a sambhur elk, the nearer tap of a woodpecker, the scream of a peacock, or the grunting of a wanderoo ape; while now and again a flock of small chattering rilawa monkeys would dart along overhead and vanish with the speed of an express train.

As we passed along our eyes were bewildered by a multitude of ferns, orchids, and climbing lilies with gaudy gold-red crowns, orange mosses and lichens, yellow purple-dashed hibiscus, whispering bamboos, brilliant convolvuli, and huge trailing lianas as thick as a ship's best hawser. We were in a true elephant country, abounding in nilloo scrub, the favourite food of that animal. This nilloo (*strobilanthes*) grows in thick sheaves with a slender stem from 6 to 20 feet long, from which shoot up handsome blue or crimson spikes of bloom, swarming with honey-bees and attracting vast numbers of rats (*Golunda Elliotti*) and jungle-fowl. The seeds are said by the natives to have the effect of blinding and stupefying the birds that feed on them.

As night fell we halted near a statue of Buddha, 54 feet high, called *Aukana-wihara*, carved out of a solid granite wall of rock at some little distance from the track, surrounded by trees gay with yellow and purple fungi. My experience at the little rest-house here will serve as a type of all such in the more out-of-the-way parts of the island. Reaching the tope of palms, and shouting "Boy" for some ten minutes, I am just beginning to wonder whether the fellow has followed the prevailing fashion and "struck," or has gone underground, when he suddenly appears from somewhere round the corner, and after hearing my wants proceeds to catch my supper. Several hours under a Ceylon sun in the jungle have made me hungry and thirsty enough to do justice to anything and everything I am likely to find put before me. In a minute or two missiles begin to roam through the air in all directions; a great commotion ensues among the poultry; long-legged hens and emaciated cocks scutter hither and thither in wild disorder; I narrowly escape being brained by a stick, which eventually knocks over a bird of unknown sex, whose dry black-boned carcase in the course of a few minutes lies before me in its native nakedness on an expanse of earthen dish. The bird, a veritable "piece of resistance," being sent up "all standing," looks as if it had not cared to live any longer and in death had found no happiness. A ghastly sight is that rooster, with its knees drawn meekly up to its breast like an American Indian mummy, while its blue-black melancholy visage seems with one eye to reproach its murderer, and with the other to survey its own unshrouded remains. This "sudden death," with a fried egg that leers at me like the eye of a gigantic albino, some sweet potatoes, pumpkin curry, and English beer, form in the aggregate a repast which brings heaven within measurable distance. Then after a smoke, on a bed that feels as if stuffed with prickly pears I essay to fall asleep, lulled by the song of mosquitoes many and the low chuckling of the night-hawk. That nothing may be wanting on the occasion to exhilarate out-wearied nature, I well remember the attentions of a vixenish hornet that dangled its legs about my ears, and looked like the ghost of an attenuated ballet-girl.

At last I have rid myself of every pest save one, a mosquito which persistently baffles me, and whose extinction I finally abandon as a hopeless task. My last waking thought is that if she can but get a drink she may settle down for the night; so I give her a big toe to worry, upon which ensues satiety on her part and a large lump on the part of my toe. Although I lose blood I gain my point, and slip off to sleep, scalping my foe at the first streak of dawn. Long before the jungle partridge has greeted the uprising sun I am on my way again, with a delicious banana and a truly filthy cup of tea inside me.

Before noon we reached the foot of a sacred hill 1000 feet high, known as Mihintala, which we climbed by a long winding staircase of 1000 steps, of which not a few are 12 and 15 feet broad. On the top stands a dagoba,[1] eighteen centuries old, from the base of which there is a magnificent view. On either hand the ocean is

[1] Dagoba, from *da*, a relic, and *geba*, a womb or receptacle.

seen gleaming afar. In front stretches a sea not of salt water but of the most brilliant foliage, broken only by the lofty dagobas of Anuradhapoora in the distance, and the shining surface of a silvery lake.

After a short halt we came down again and went along the remaining eight miles to our destination between mouldering walls and fragments of fallen columns, a veritable Buddhist *Via Sacra*. At the present time almost overgrown with jungle, this road was formerly kept in good repair, and on great festivals was covered by a carpet spread the whole distance from Mihintala to the city, in order that the pilgrims when purified in the bath might reach the shrine with unsoiled feet. Half-way we forded a small stream, then jogged onwards through dense woods in stifling heat, and came at last to the few scattered dwellings that are now the only habitable remains of a city which once covered 256 square miles.

Hot were we, indeed, and inexpressibly weary when we reached our goal, nor did we stir a foot from the rest-house until we had bathed and fortified ourselves with a meal consisting of fowls cut up and boiled with onions, chillies, rice, and potato shavings, seasoned with salt and pepper, to which in a moment of true culinary inspiration I added with excellent effect my last tin of soup. Then we turned our steps to the ruins of the *Lowa-maha-paya*, or palace of brass, consisting of 1600 granite columns each a yard thick and twice the height of a man, and many of them still standing erect. In its original state the building, where now sunshine and shadow sleep upon silent floors, was roofed with polished brass, and consisted of a square with sides 234 feet long, nine storeys high, and containing upon each floor 100 rooms. Robert Knox, who was for many years a captive in Ceylon, says of it: "They say ninety kings have reigned here, the spirits of whom they hold to be now saints in glory, having merited it by making pagodas and stone pillars and images to the honour of their gods, whereof there are many yet remaining. . . . Near by is a river,[1] over which there have been three stone bridges built upon stone pillars, but now are thrown down, and the country all desolate without inhabitants."

Hard by are a royal tomb, a royal crematory, a

[1] The Malwatoya, *oya* meaning *water*; compare the *ouwa* of Abyssinia and the French *eau*.

royal place of wailing, a priests' assembly hall, and the Peacock palace. But the crowning glory of Anuradhapoora is the sacred Bo-tree (*Ficus religiosa*), famous, apart from its lingering sanctity, as being beyond doubt the oldest known tree in the world. To this "illustrious, victorious, supreme lord," as it is called in the native annals, must yield in point of antiquity the baobab of Senegal, the gum-tree of Gippsland, the dragon-tree of Orotava,[1] the Wellingtōnia of California, the chestnut of Etna, the oak of Windsor, the yew of Fountains, the cedar of Soma, the olive of Gethsemane. As I look at it I am reminded that it was planted B.C. 288 by Devenipiatissa, so that it is now 2179 years old. There are many trees of great age on the earth, whose extreme antiquity is a matter of more or less doubt; but none of those mentioned above are in the proper sense of the word sacred trees, none of them are actual objects of veneration as is this bo-tree at Anuradhapoora, the wood of which has never been touched by steel, and whose leaves as they fall to the ground are reverently gathered up and eagerly sought after by pilgrims.

[1] Note G.

According to the Buddhist belief this tree was originally a branch of the one under which Gautama was resting at the time of his apotheosis or death, and near which afterwards stood the city of Buddha Gaya, at one time a large and flourishing place, but described by Fa Hian in the fifth century as deserted. It is said by the Singhalese to have occupied, like the Delphi of the Greeks, the exact centre of the earth. As the bo-tree is sacred to Gautama Buddha, so is the banyan to his predecessor, and so is the *na* or iron-wood tree destined to be to the next and last Buddha.

In the annals of the year 459 this tree is spoken of as "the monarch of the forest, endowed with miraculous powers, which has stood for ages, promoting the spiritual welfare of the people and the spread of true religion." By each successive dynasty records of its exact age have been religiously kept, extracts from which may be seen at the end of Sir Emerson Tennent's valuable work on Ceylon. It stands in a court 340 feet long and 214 wide, its branches straggling half over the place, supported here and there by masonry work. The leaf very much resembles a large ace of spades with a long tendril growing from the point. Out of respect to the sage it has "always an apparent motion, whether there be wind stirring or not"; just as in Syria they say that the cross of Christ was made of the aspen, which ever since has trembled.

The temple is a plain building, but contains a few excellent antique carvings, notably on the threshold, which is decorated with the lotus, and various animals, including, strange to say, the unicorn. There is the creature plain enough, head, body, and limbs of a horse with a tusk-shaped horn. The natives, who call it *Kangewana*, aver that once it was common in real life, against which statement must be set the fact that no remains have ever been found. But it is, to say the least, curious that there should have been represented by those ancient craftsmen an animal the form of which exactly corresponds with a creature looked upon in modern times as ideal.[1]

Here also are richly ornamented capitals, balus-

[1] Jerome Lobo, a Jesuit who visited Abyssinia in the seventeenth century, says: "Here has been seen the unicorn, that beast so much talked of and so little known; the prodigious swiftness with which this creature runs from one wood to another has given me no opportunity of examining it particularly, yet I have had so near a sight of it as to be able to give some description of it. The shape is the same with that of a beautiful horse, exact and

trades, and bas-reliefs, of foliage and animals less mythical than the twin supporter of the royal arms of England. The goose holds a conspicuous place, as it does on all Buddhist monuments, a bird ever held in high veneration among men of all countries. It is still the national emblem on the flag of Burmah, where the people, like the Egyptians of old, cut their weights to the figure of the bird.[1] According to Julius Cæsar it was once considered in Britain an impious act to eat a goose, and similar ideas can be traced among nations widely separated. Here at Anuradhapoora its effigy is carved in a fashion that has little in common with the crudeness of modern native work ; in a museum you might easily mistake it for Greek workmanship, as also the beautifully wrought foliage pattern upon a semicircular slab of stone at the foot of a staircase. There must have been both wealth and taste to produce such work.

How difficult is it now for the imagination to repeople the deserted streets of Anuradhapoora,

nicely proportioned, of a bay colour, with a black tail, which in some provinces is long, in others very short ; some have long manes hanging to the ground. They are so timorous that they never feed but surrounded with other beasts that defend them."

[1] The most ancient painted picture in the world is a picture of pasturing geese found at Maydoum, and now in the new Museum at Gizeh in Egypt.

of which the chief one was once lined with 11,000 houses! 2000 years ago the city was gay with gardens and public baths; the pageantry of many a royal and religious procession flashed along its ways; there were fine shops and crowded bazaars, dancing-halls and music saloons, rest-houses, almshouses, hospitals for animals and men. A contemporary native writer thus describes the scene: "The golden pinnacles of temples and palaces glitter in the sky, the streets are spanned by many arches, the sideways strewn with black sand, the middle with white; on either side stand vases holding flowers, and niches with statues for lamp-bearers. In the thoroughfares are to be seen throngs of men who are armed with bows and arrows. Among these people are many of lofty stature, who carry large swords; the strength of these godlike beings is so great that with one blow of their mighty weapon they can sever the body of an elephant. Myriads of people, elephants, horses, bullocks, palanquins, and hackeries are constantly passing and re-passing. Among this busy multitude devoted to occupation may be found many who make the pleasure of others their employment, as there are necromancers, dancers, and musicians of far-off nations, whose chank-shells and tom-toms are ornamented with cloth of gold. The gates of the city are far asunder; the distance of the principal gate to the southern entrance is four gaws,[1] and from the northern to the southern gate is it not also four gaws? The principal streets are three; their names are Great King Street, Great River Street, and Moon Street; in the latter are more than twice 5000 dwellings, the greater number being goodly-sized houses. The lesser streets in this vast city are countless. The king's palace is a stupendous edifice and has immense ranges of buildings, some of two and three storeys in height. The subterranean apartments are of great extent. What man can tell the space of ground they cover?"

The Hon. G. Turnour in his edition of the *Màhawanso* thus translates a description of the consecration of a site for a temple at Anuradhapoora by Devenipiatissa in B.C. 307: "When the monarch was about to define the limits of a garden that he intended to devote to the priesthood, he approached the priests worthy of

[1] *i.e.* sixteen miles.

veneration, and bowed down to them; and then proceeding with them to the upper ferry of the river, he made his progress, ploughing the ground with a golden plough. The superb state elephants, Mahapadumo and Kunjaro, having been harnessed to the golden plough, Devenipiatissa, accompanied by the priests and attended by his army, himself holding the shaft, defined the line of boundary. Surrounded by vases exquisitely painted, which were carried in procession, and by gorgeous flags tinkling with the bells attached to them; sprinkled with red sandal dust, guarded by gold and silver staves, the concourse decorated with mirrors of glittering glass and with garlands, and with baskets borne down by the weight of flowers; triumphal arches made of plantain trees, and females holding up umbrellas and other decorations; excited by the symphony of every description of music, encompassed by the martial might of his empire; overwhelmed by the shouts of gratitude and festivity which welcomed him from the four quarters of the earth;—this lord of the land made his progress, ploughing amidst enthusiastic acclamations, hundreds of waving handkerchiefs, and the exultation produced by the presenting of superb offerings."

Fa Hian, who was at Anuradhapoora in the fifth century, mentions that he saw there among many other marvels an image of blue jasper, 23½ feet in height, sparkling with precious stones, and holding a very large pearl in its hand. Another Chinese traveller speaks of the city as being the residence of many magistrates, grandees, and foreign merchants, the mansions beautiful, the public buildings richly adorned, and "houses for preaching built at every thoroughfare." The population seems to have been about 3,000,000, of whom we are told that 420,000 were fighting men. Now what is there? The far from stately dwelling of a Government official, a few priests' houses, a poverty-stricken bazaar, and a handful of palm-thatched huts. To such desolation has fallen the sacred capital of the Kingdom of Lions! One principal cause of its decline seems to have been the inability or unwillingness of the people to keep the tanks in repair, in consequence of which the place became unhealthy; many died, others sought a dwelling-place elsewhere, and its ruin was completed by an invasion of Tamuls.

Within a few hundred yards of the Brazen Palace stand several mighty dagobas, huge brick erections, in shape something between a pyramid and a pagoda. Of these the most celebrated are the *Ruanwellé* (gold-dust) and the *Thuparamaya.* The former, a very mountain of masonry, 150 feet high, standing on a well-preserved terrace, was built by Gaimono B.C. 150, and crowned by Singha in A.D. 243 with a pinnacle of glass as a protection against lightning. The Thuparamaya was built four centuries earlier by Tisso I., for the reception of Buddha's collar-bone, and was surrounded by slender pillars and ornaments "like the gems round the throat of a youthful matron." The pillars still remaining are in four lines of twenty-six each, 21 feet high, with round capitals, octagonal shafts, and square bases; they are ornamented with very delicate and minute chiselwork, and are so arranged upon the granite platform as to form the radii of a circle of which the dagoba is the centre.

The *Jaitawanarama* dagoba (A.D. 310) was once 315 feet in height, but is now reduced to 269.

The *Abhayagiri* (B.C. 87) was built by Walagambahu to commemorate his victory over the Tamuls, and stood originally 405 feet in height (40 feet higher than the cross on St. Paul's Cathedral), which time has reduced to 240. This vast structure is no less than 360 feet in diameter, its contents being calculated at 20,000,000 cubic feet, material enough to build a city the size of Coventry, or to make a wall from London to Edinburgh 1 foot thick and 10 feet high. It has been estimated that the building of it nowadays would occupy 500 men for seven years. The brickwork is still smooth and compact and the edges are unworn. In the mortar you can trace remnants of the burnt pearl shells, and the *chunam* coating upon the walls still preserves its angularity and polish.

Dagobas were usually hemispherical, this form being probably chosen as being best calculated to resist the inroads of vegetable growth. Their similarity to the ancient central American edifices is remarkable; the shape and size of dome, the small tower on the summit, the vegetation that abounds in every nook and cranny, the style of ornamentation, the small entrance at the base, all serve to complete the resemblance. When

Gaimono was about to build the Ruanwellé dagoba he asked a mason what shape it was to be. The man filled a gold dish with water, and taking some in the palm of his hand caused a bubble like a coral bead to rise on the surface. Then he said to the king, "In this shape will I build it."[1]

All the dagobas, like the rest of the ruins at Anuradhapoora, are covered with a dense mass of vegetable growth, trees, shrubs, and creepers, showing how futile are man's most determined efforts to resist the attacks of time, and how powerful are the effects of the silent forces of nature. Ages ago a bird of the air dropped the seed of a bo-tree upon yonder temple or tower. There where it fell it germinated, and little by little penetrated in search of moisture and support. The tree had to live somehow upon that bare ruin, and it did live, and with its roots during the course of centuries it has riven asunder the mass of solid masonry.

The country for many miles round these dagobas is covered with architectural remains, most of them entirely overgrown. The soil is in many places red with brick-dust and strewn with pedestals and sarcophagi, mixed up with

[1] Note H.

maimed figures of bulls and broken elephants in stone, far less objectionable in their helpless quiescence than the myriads of living and thirsting winged pests with which the surrounding jungle teems.[1]

We need not marvel at the utter destruction on every side. In a climate like that of the plains of Ceylon a very short time is enough for an incredible mass of vegetation to spring up. The neglect of a few days will render a path or a doorway impassable. Can we wonder then at the present state of Anuradhapoora after the lapse of so many centuries? The city has vanished like a dream; its courts are the dwelling-place of owls, its palaces are mingled with the dust; the roaming jackal cannot find a bone of all the multitudes who lived and feasted and sorrowed and died in them. The giant images still sit as they sat when thronging thousands bowed daily before them, the same vacant unearthly look upon their stony faces; the dagoba still divides the sapphire sky and casts the self-same shadow as of old. But where are the hands which reared it, the men who sought its shelter in the burning heat of noon? Where are the last year's snows?

[1] Note I.

CHAPTER VI

RIVERS AND MOUNTAINS: ADAM'S PEAK

Turn eastward now thine eyes, and in the sunlight bold
The Samanala peak, that sacred rock, behold,
Where, with his goddess train, great Samana ador'd
Th' illustrious lotus Footprint of Buddha, Omniscient Lord.

CEYLON is a land well watered by streams and springs, fed by the heavy monsoon rains, and the frequent showers which are caused by the interception of ocean vapours by the high mountains of the interior. Of the larger rivers the majority follow a tortuous course in the direction of south, south-east, and west, taking their rise in the lofty inland table-lands, and hurrying impetuously over many rapids and cataracts along ravines and precipitous defiles. As they near the sea the current grows more sluggish in channels which open out between thick groves of screw pines, mangroves, and tamarisks, amongst whose roots lie many lazy crocodiles. At the time of the wet monsoon the streams are subject to sudden and extensive floods, rising sometimes to a height of 30 feet in a very few hours. Some years ago the Kalani Ganga, which enters the sea near Colombo, and forms a picturesque feature just outside the city on the road leading to the celebrated Kalani temple, overflowed its banks and swept away hundreds of houses, together with a bridge of boats, which has since been replaced by a very substantial structure of the same type. As a natural result of these inundations an immense quantity of slime and moisture is deposited over the low-lying lands, which under the tropical sun produces no small amount of malarial disease.

The largest river in the island is the Mahawellé Ganga, which after rising in the southern range makes a very fine cataract at Rambody, in shape like the Hönefos in Norway, and after many rapids turns sharp to the east near Kandy and then to the north. It then breaks up into numerous branches, and finally at the end of 134 miles reaches the sea 25 miles south of Trincomalee on the east coast, the well-known naval station with one of the finest harbours in the world. Second in importance is the Kalani

Ganga, rising in the north-east of Adam's Peak and flowing for 84 miles westward to the sea north of Colombo. The Kalu Ganga is the picturesque stream to the south of the Peak that skirts the city of Ratnapoora, the capital of the ruby district; while the Maha-oya and the Wallaway (each 70 miles long), together with a few others useless for navigable purposes on account of their frequent rapids, make up about a dozen streams each exceeding 50 miles in length.

These rivers, added to the springs which abound almost everywhere, were grand sources of supply to the ancient inhabitants, who made use of them for the purpose of filling their artificial tanks and watercourses. The energies of the early kings, especially those of the Wijayo dynasty in the fifth and sixth centuries before Christ, were devoted to the construction of tanks, many of which even in their present ruinous condition excite the wonder of the traveller. Not a few of them are of enormous size, and are the more astonishing when we know what the native tools and appliances of those times were, and remember that these vast reservoirs are the result of the sheer toil and suffering perseverance of tens of thousands of busy human hands. The largest tank is that of Kalawera, near Damboola, which I have already mentioned, made in the fifth century, and in its perfect state not less than 40 miles in circumference, 12 miles of which were embanked with solid stone. Another in a low marshy tract at Minery, 20 miles round, was formed by throwing a dam across the Kara Ganga channel. Although in the construction of the vast embankments labour was often, from want of scientific knowledge, uselessly expended, the natives must have gained for themselves some renown as workmen, for we read that in the eighth century the Raja of Kashmir sent to Ceylon for engineers to build tanks for him. With the single exception of the tanks at Aden, there are no more remarkable works of the kind in the world, for neither Lake Mœris, which, notwithstanding the statements of Herodotus and Pliny, is now considered to have been a vast natural depression, nor the Mogul tanks near Delhi, are equal to these truly colossal achievements. Most of them unfortunately have long ago fallen into ruin, but of late years the Government has with considerable energy taken in hand the work of restoration. In the present state of the island not a few of them would be useless for the purpose of irrigation, seeing that the extent of land which they would serve would be out of all proportion to the cost of their maintenance.

The mountainous districts of Ceylon, as distinct from the loftier individual summits, average in height from 800 to 5000 feet, and over an area of some 4000 square miles in the south and west exhibit very great variety of form with but few solitary peaks, and culminate in the dome-shaped mass of Pedrutallagalla (8280 feet), the loftiest in the island. The sides of the mountains are invariably steep, and in many instances exceedingly precipitous. There are no lakes or stagnant waterholes to be found in the ranges, but every valley has its own outlet, with a gradual though irregular descent from highlands to sea-level. Some of these valleys, as, for instance, that of Maturalla, are from 3000 to 4000 feet deep, with a width not exceeding half a mile.

The general geological features of the Adam Peak range are thus described by Dr. Hochstetter, the eminent geologist: "The chief direction," he says, "is from south-south-east to north-north-west, corresponding with the chief direction of the strata of the gneiss of which they are composed. The gneiss is uniformly of a species not often met with, studded with garnets, and between the strata are inserted single beds of hornblende gneiss and splinters of pure hornblende, as also granulite gneiss and pure granulite. The steep final cone of the rock consists of a granulitic gneiss of varying texture, from coarse to fine, and abounding in garnets; everywhere, even up to the highest summit, the gneiss is decomposed on the surface into laterite products. The huge blocks of brown ironstone, however, which are found near the summit in the hollow path, may owe their origin to the decomposition of the hornblende."

It is to be noted that there are in Ceylon no traces whatever either of violent geological changes or of any fossil remains, with the exception of a few tusks, bones, and shells that have been dug up beneath the level of the bed of the Kalu Ganga. Throughout the whole island the geological formation is singularly uniform (except in the Jaffna district), consisting either of primitive rocks or their *débris*. The species are few, the most abundant being gneiss or granite, with here and there, as at Trincomalee, quartz rock, hornblende, and dolomite. A fine-grained gray granite is met with near Galle in the south, but taking the island throughout, by far the most frequent species is a gneiss consisting of white felspar and quartz in a pure crystalline state, with layers of black mica, or mica slate, and many crystals of a bright-coloured garnet scattered through it. At Trincomalee, in the north-east, there is a very picturesque ridge of milk-white quartz quite bare and standing erect like denuded veins. From its precipitous character it presents the appearance of a building in ruins, and is known as Chapel Point. Farther north a good deal of limestone occurs with abundant shells embedded, while at intervals all round the coast sandstone well adapted for building purposes is found, like a broken chain, lying between high and low water mark.[1]

What Fuji San is to Japan that is Samanella or Adam's Peak to Ceylon. If Sinai and Olivet and the holy places at Jerusalem be of supreme and abiding interest to the Christian

[1] The vertical rise of the tide round Ceylon is about 3 feet, the same as at St. Helena.

world, what shall we say of a mountain which at the present moment is a central point in the superstitious veneration of 800,000,000 of our fellow-men? On its lofty cone year by year, in the month of April, thousands of pilgrims from the shadows of the Himalayas, the banks of the Indus, the marshes of the Irawadi, the burning plains of Persia, the stony wastes of Arabia, and the teeming cities of China, prostrate themselves before that which is to a Christian eye a singularly insignificant object of worship. In a hollow indentation of the lonely peak the Brahman and the Buddhist lay their offerings of flowers, and the Moslem casts his gifts of gold, in honour of Adam, or Buddha, or Siva. There are many mountains of twice the height of Adam's Peak, many upon whose mightier masses of eternal snow the eye gazes with a more rapt admiration; but nowhere does there rise from earth towards heaven one that more deeply moves the heart and stirs the soul than this "landmark in the sea of time," renowned through the ages no less for its bold and striking form than for the multitude of those traditions which gather, like its own clouds, around its head.

The mountain is known among the Singhalese as Samanella, the hill of Samana, or as Hammanelle Sri-pada, the hill of the sacred footstep. Bryant in his *Analysis of Antient Mythology* (1767) has the following remarks: "The Pike of Adam is properly the summit sacred to Ad Ham, the king or deity Ham, the Amon of Egypt. This is plain to demonstration, from another name given to it by the Singhalese who live near the mountain, and call it Ham-al-el; this without any change is Ham-eel-el, or Ham the Sun, and relates to the antient religion of the island. In short, everything in these countries savours of Chaldaic and Egyptian institution." Although this tracing back of the sanctity of the Peak to the worship of Ammon may be pronounced incorrect, seeing that Hamaleel is nothing but a Dutch corruption of the native name, Bryant was perfectly accurate in stating that many of the doctrines and sciences of Egypt were in old times imported from the banks of the Nile into India. But if the theory he advances in the foregoing extract were a true one, it was surely to be expected that at least some traces would have been found in some form or other of the ancient religion and worship to which he alludes. But none such have ever come to light; nor is there anything peculiar in the mode of worship as now practised on the Peak: Samana is there worshipped just like any other Hindoo deity, and the cult of the Sri-pada or sacred footprint differs not at all from the ordinary cult of Sakya Muni or of Siva.

Fantastic local legends give to the origin of the mountain's sacred character a date earlier than the sober historian will be prepared to accept. The priest in charge of the Sri-pada tells you that King Walagambahu (B.C. 104), when driven from his throne by Malabar invaders,[1] wandered about for more than fourteen years, living in caves among the mountains. One day, when roaming near the foot of Samanella, he saw a deer which, being hungry, he resolved to kill; but on giving it chase he found it was impossible to come up with it, and by degrees the animal led him by steep and difficult ways to the top of the mountain, where he was the first of mortals to look upon the footprint of Buddha, and where by a supernatural revelation the everlasting sanctity of the spot was made

[1] See *ante*, p. 27.

known to him. This was the same monarch who, after his restoration, erected the famous Abhayagiri dagoba at Anuradhapoora, and in B.C. 88 brought together 500 of the most learned priests to a cave at Matale, where for the first time the tenets of the Buddhistic faith were reduced to writing.

A curious side-light is thrown upon the antiquity of the mountain shrine by the fact that in the Samaritan version of the Septuagint the word *Sarendib* is found in Genesis viii. 4, instead of Ararat, as being the place whereon Noah's ark rested after the deluge. This manuscript version was brought to Europe from Damascus by an Italian in the early part of the seventeenth century, and though said by the Samaritans themselves to have been written B.C. 20 by one of their own priests, is usually assigned to a much later date. The manuscript contains, in common with most old Targums or paraphrases, many variations from the original text, and in the passage referred to is quite in harmony with the common oriental belief that the waters of the deluge did not reach to the top of Adam's Peak; from which theory some have deduced its sanctity as a virgin relic of the world before the flood.

While not presuming to express an opinion on such a knotty point, I may draw attention to the *dictum* of the learned M. Figuier, who as a scientist affirms the age of the Peak to be greater than that of either Ararat or the Himalayas, and that it was towering over the Southern Ocean at a period when Europe lay half submerged.

We stand upon firmer ground when we record that in A.D. 24 a certain Meghavahana, king of Kashmir, made an expedition to Ceylon for the express purpose of visiting the mountain, which was at that date, so far as we know, called simply the "mountain of gems," with no mention either of Adam or Buddha. A yet more illustrious visitor, according to some, was the great Macedonian conqueror, whose voyage to Serendib and devotions at the sepulchre of Adam are narrated by the imaginative pen of the Persian poet Ashreef in the fifteenth century. Unfortunately, seeing that the adulatory bard makes one of Alexander's companions to be a man who did not live till many years afterwards, there is some reason for taking exception to the belief that the foot of the youthful master of the world ever trod the sacred heights of Samanella.

I have already stated that Asiatics of all creeds vie with each other in their veneration of the Peak. The Arab and the Moorman behold in the footprint the impress of the foot of the first father of mankind, who is, according to the precepts of the Koran, held by them in the highest honour. The Buddhist, on the other hand, when he has accomplished the arduous ascent, has no eye but for that memento of his incarnation, which Sakya Muni, the fourth Buddha, left for the veneration of his disciples when he deigned for a while to make his resting-place here. It is of interest to look at each of these beliefs for a moment. In accordance with the Mohammedan tradition, Adam, who, they say, was of the height of a tall palm, here set his foot for the last time before he went up into heaven. It was a very early belief that after his expulsion from Eden he found a refuge in Ceylon, and at one time there must have been a structure on the top of the mountain which passed either for his dwelling or his tomb, for Marignolli in the fourteenth century wrote: "When Adam was expelled from Eden, an angel took him by the arm and set him down on this mountain in Seyllan, and by chance Adam placed his right foot on the stone, which still retains the impression; at the same time Eve was placed on another mountain four days' journey distant." And in another place he says, "That high mountain has a pinnacle of great height which can rarely be seen for the clouds. But in pity for our tears God lighted it up one day ere the sun rose, so that we saw it shining as with the brightest flame. In the way down from this mountain there is a fine level spot, still at a great height, and there you find in order: firstly, the mark of Adam's foot; secondly, a certain statue of a sitting figure with the left hand resting on the knee, and the right hand raised towards the west; lastly, there is the house of Adam, which he made with his own hands of an oblong quadrangular shape like a sepulchre, with a door in the middle, formed of great slabs of marble, not cemented but laid one upon another; and as the deluge never mounted so high it was never disturbed."

In the Koran (cap. 2) we read: "Satan caused them to forfeit Paradise, and turned them out of the state of happiness wherein they had been: wherefore we said, Get ye down, the one of you an enemy unto the other; and there shall be a dwelling-place for you on earth, and a provision for a season." Which Sale annotates thus: "When they were cast down from Paradise Adam fell in the isle of Ceylon or Serendib, and Eve near Jeddah in Arabia, and after a separation of two hundred years Adam was on his repentance conducted by the angel Gabriel to a mountain near Mecca, where he found his wife, with whom he retired to Ceylon." There he is considered to have remained standing on one foot until by many years of penance he had wholly expiated his transgression; and he left this footprint which may with truth be said to have been fashioned out of the sorrow of his soul. Sir Thomas Herbert, not to be outdone by those who tell us that, like the tears of the Nereids in the Cyclades which turned to pearls, the tears of Adam became gems, speaks of a (non-existent) lake on the Peak, which was formed by the tears of "our first forefather" when he heard the news of the death of Abel; to which a Moslem writer adds that the tears of the right eye caused the flowing of the river Euphrates, and those of the left the Tigris. Such traditions as these probably come from a Gnostic source. Mohammedan travellers visiting the island, and hearing of the footprint there, assigned it without inquiry to Adam. Who does not remember the charming tale of Sinbad, who tells us that in his sixth voyage he visited the capital of Serendib? which, he records, "stands at the end of a fine valley in the midst of the island encompassed by high mountains, seen three days off at sea. I made," he adds, "by way of devotion a pilgrimage to the place where Adam was confined after his banishment from Paradise, and had the curiosity to go to the top of the mountain."[1]

Marco Polo, writing in 1295, speaks of the Peak as if it contained the grave and not the footmark of Adam. "In this island," writes the famous Venetian, "there is an exceeding high mountain; it rises right up so steep and precipitous that no one could ascend it, were it not that they have taken and fixed to it several great and massive iron chains, so disposed that by help of these men are able to mount to the top. And I tell you they say that in this mountain is the sepulchre

[1] Note J.

of Adam our first parent; at least that is what the Saracens say. But the Idolaters say that it is the sepulchre of Sagamoni Borcan,[1] before whose time there were no idols." He goes on to narrate how the golden image of Sagamoni made by his royal father was "the first idol that the idolaters ever had," who "come thither on pilgrimage from very long distances and with great devotion, just as Christians go to the shrine of Messer Saint James in Gallicia. And they maintain that the monument on the mountain is that of the king's son, according to the story I have been telling you; and that the teeth and the hairs and the dish that are there were those of the same king's son. But the Saracens say that the teeth and the hairs and the dish were those of Adam. Whose they were in truth, God knoweth. Howbeit, according to the Holy Scripture of the Church, the sepulchre of Adam is not in that part of the world. Now it befel that the Great Kaan heard how on that mountain there was the sepulchre of our first father Adam, and that some of his hair and of his teeth, and

[1] *i.e.* Sakya Muni or Gautama Buddha, with the affix Burkhan, meaning "divinity."

the dish from which he used to eat, were still preserved there. So he thought he would get hold of them somehow or another, and despatched a great embassy for the purpose in the year of Christ 1284. The ambassadors, with a great company, travelled on by sea and by land until they arrived at the island of Seilan, and presented themselves before the king. And they were so urgent with him that they succeeded in getting two of the grinder teeth which were passing great and thick, and they also got some of the hair, and the dish from which that personage used to eat, which is of a very beautiful green porphyry.[1] And when they had returned to their lord he was passing glad, and ordered all the ecclesiastics and others to go forth to meet these reliques, which he was led to believe were those of Adam. In sooth, the whole population of Cambaluc went forth to meet them, and the ecclesiastics took them over and carried them to the Great Kaan, who received them with great joy and reverence."[2]

As early as the second century the pilgrims voyaging from China to India used to gaze with

[1] See *ante*, p. 68.

[2] *Travels of Marco Polo* (Yule's translation), Bk. iii. cap. 15.

awe upon the lofty peak towering into the sky, of which the Portuguese Ribeiro (1685) says that "it is twenty leagues from the sea, and seamen see it twenty leagues from the land; it is two miles high." In the religious books of China we find reverent notices of the sacred footprint of "the first created man," who is called Pawn-koo, and also statements of the popular belief that in the hollow of his foot there lies a small quantity of pure water which never dries up all the year round.

As for the legends connecting the footprint of Buddha with the mountain, they must be acknowledged to be of comparatively recent date. The old Buddhistic sacred books show no knowledge of them, and I have found no earlier mention of them than that of the Chinese traveller Fa Hian, who was in Ceylon A.D. 413, and stayed for some time in Anuradhapoora. He writes that "by the strength of his divine foot Foe (Buddha) left the print of one of his feet to the north of the royal city, and the print of the other on the summit of a mountain." As Fa Hian has left no record of a personal visit to the holy mount, it is more than probable that at that time it was not such an object of reverent attraction as it has since become. There is a trustworthy account of a pilgrimage to it in the ninth century, and of similar expeditions, by Prakrama Bahu I. (1150) and Prakrama Bahu III. 200 years later.

Four Buddhas have visited the Peak.[1] The first was there B.C. 3001, the second B.C. 2099, the third B.C. 1014, and the fourth, Sakya Muni or Gautama, B.C. 577. The latter is said on one occasion to have planted one foot on the mountain-top and the other on the coast of Madura in India, causing thereby such a disruption of the "elements," that the island has ever since been separated from the mainland. We are by this feat irresistibly reminded of Bolster, Thomas Hood's Cornishman, who took a similar stride from one hill-top to another, though fortunately with less drastic results. I cannot refrain from transcribing the following curious exordium, written about A.D. 400, and bearing on this subject: "One Boodhoo,[2] who acquired Nirvane; who came into the world like other Boodhoos; from whom is derived the food of life [*i.e.* religion];

[1] Of the five Buddhas four have already appeared on earth and attained the state of *Nirvana*; the last, *Nitre*, is yet to come.

[2] *i.e.* Buddha, from a Pali word signifying "wisdom."

who is celebrated for his thirty-two great manly beauties, and for the eighty-two signs connected with them, and for the light which shines a fathom round his body, and for the beams of light that dart from the top of his head; who is the preceptor of three worlds; who is acquainted with the past, present, and future; who during four *asankeas* of *kalpes* so conducted himself as to be an example of the thirty great qualities; who subdued Mareya and his attendants, and became Boodhoo:—in the eighth year from that event he rose into the air, spread beams of light of six different colours round his person, and stamped the impression of his foot, bearing the noble marks Chakkra-lak-sana, and the 108 auspicious tokens, on the rock Samanta-koota-parwate;—which is celebrated for the cold and lovely waters of its rivers, for its mountain torrents, and for its flowery groves, spreading in the air their sweet-scented pollen; which is the crown of the Virgin island, rich in mines of all kinds of precious stones, like a maid decked with jewels."

There are other memories of a different kind which cling to the mountain. The Brahman calls it Sivanolipadam, and claims the footprint as that of Siva the destroyer. At the coming of the Hindoo conquerors they found that the Peak had been long held in reverence by all true believers. Fakirs from beyond the Ganges found growing in the clefts of its ravines the same simples that they were familiar with on the slopes of the Himalayas, the favourite dwelling-place of Siva. In the glens and glades of Samanella they searched, just as men search now, for the plant *Sansevi*, or tree of life. The place was known among them as the "ascent to heaven"; and as all who are destined by Siva to eternal bliss receive on their heads the impress of his sacred foot, it was by no obscure process of transmutation that the Sri-pada came to be looked upon as a memorial of his presence. Christians, on the other hand, with greater acerbity, have wrangled over it as a relic either of Queen Candace's eunuch, or of his spiritual father Saint Thomas. What the Ethiopian nobleman had to do with the Peak I have not been able to ascertain, but in the case of the apostle the tradition seems to have grown out of the fact that in a quarry near Colombo there was once found a stone with a mark on it which was said to be very much like the impression of the apostolic knee at Meliapoor. *Voilà comment on écrit l'histoire!*

At the time of the second Buddha's visit, twenty centuries before the apostolic age, the Peak was already known as Samanta-koota or peak of Samana, brother of that Rama who in B.C. 2386 is said to have subdued the island. Indeed Samana, or, as he is also called, Lackshmana, is to this hour looked upon as the real guardian deity or *dewa* of the Peak, in whose honour there are two shrines: one on the summit, and at the base, near Ratnapoora, a statelier one, surrounded by peepul or bo-trees, with a huge pair of elephant's tusks at the door, and within his yellow effigy, together with his golden bow and arrow; moreover, the superb groves of giant rhododendrons which clothe the eastern steeps of the mountain with a robe of brilliant scarlet are dedicated to him. The legend runs that Samana, having heard of the coming of Buddha to Ceylon, requested him to leave the impress of his foot upon the mountain of which he was the spiritual guardian. In the midst of the assembled *dewas*, Buddha, looking towards the east, made the impression of his foot, "in length three inches less than the cubit of the carpenter, and the impress remains as a seal to show that Lanka (Ceylon) is the inheritance of Buddha, and that his religion will here flourish."

Although at the present moment there is not anywhere on earth a similar vestige of antique faith which is the object of so great veneration as the Sri-pada, I may remind my reader that Adam, if he was the first, was by no means the only man of mark to make a permanent impression upon the actual physical surface of the globe. Our old friend Herodotus, who has come unharmed through so many fires of doubt and ridicule, asserts that he beheld with his own eyes a gigantic footprint of Hercules on a rock in Scythia, which seems to have escaped the notice of later travellers. At Damascus, in the Great Mosque, a stone is pointed out as bearing the impress of the foot of Moses. At Behar in Southern India you can ascertain if you will the exact size of the foot of Saint Thomas from the impression he made on a harder material than that of the hearts of his converts. Under the shadows of Etna, in the beautiful Piazza dei Martiri at Catania, stands a fair statue of the youthful martyr Saint Agatha, who left the imprint of her foot in the neighbouring church of S. Carcere, built over her prison-house. In Mexico the intrepid and unfortunate Emperor Montezuma has left his mark upon a slab of solid porphyry. At a village near Bangkok in Siam there is a similar relic, but whose I know not; to say nothing of the sacred hollow at Jerusalem in the chapel of the Ascension that stands on the site of the ancient church of Helena.[1]

The ascent of Adam's Peak is more arduous than that of any mountain of the same altitude with which I am acquainted. Not only is the walking terribly rough and steep in many places, to say nothing of the trapeze-like performances one has to go through on the loose hanging chains near the top, but there is great exhaustion consequent upon the stifling heat in the jungle country through which the track lies for the first few hours. This, added to the general difficulties of the climb and the intolerable presence of hordes of bloodthirsty land leeches, made up an amount of discomfort and fatigue more than enough to dissuade me from ever making a second attempt.

[1] Note K.

One morning in January, long before daylight, I started from Ratnapoora, a town some forty miles from Colombo, lying in a green plain on the right bank of the Kalu Ganga, surrounded by finely wooded mountains. Passing out into low jungle land, the mere thought of what the heat in such a place would be like when the sun was abroad was enough to make me quicken my steps so as to reach the higher ground as soon as possible. Even as it was, the light clothing I wore seemed to be a superfluity, and I envied my coolie his naked back and shoeless feet. Before half a mile had been traversed I was in a condition bordering upon dissolution; and seeing that I was in no very robust health at the time, I am quite sure that if I had known what lay before me I should have feebly succumbed early in the day, and should have left to an abler pen the pleasant task of trying to give to others some idea of those later experiences which, when I had reached Ratnapoora again in safety, repaid me a thousandfold for all risks and fatigue.

The path lay through myriads of convolvuli, pitcher-plants, orchids, and dwarf-bamboos, with a thousand other floral beauties not to be distinguished in the light of the moon, which hung like an ivory sickle low in the west. A mile from the city we passed the Balangodde *wihara*, perched on a height above the river, and embowered amid trees and creeper-clad rocks. Another 3 or 4 miles (which I could well believe to have been ten) brought us to Gillemalle, a very romantic spot on a diminutive plateau half a mile long, flanked by palm groves and hills robed in every tint of greenery, but looking dull and dim through the hot misty night air. From this point we pushed on along a rapidly mounting track until the first streaks of dawn shot upwards over the eastern hills, and in a very little while all was bright burning day. At every step now we rose above a fairer and fairer scene, fighting our way through giant creepers, clambering across ravines and multitudinous crags with the brawling Kalu Ganga at their foot, till we called a halt at Palabadula (1500 feet), where we left the leeches behind us, and after our 8 miles' tramp were conscious of certain cravings of the inner man that would no longer take denial. We made a hasty breakfast in the *ambalam* or rest-house, and inspected the *wihara*, containing a rude copper model of the sacred footprint, said to be a facsimile of the golden one that used to be on the summit. It is possible to ride up the mountain as far as Palabadula, but beyond, for the rest of the ascent, there is no way for anything on four legs less nimble than a goat or a chamois. To the top from here is 6250 feet, but by the pilgrim path over 10 miles, the first part of which lies along the edge of scarped cliffs, down which you can hear the clatter of a falling stone long after it has passed from sight. I saw no more lianas and trailing parasites, but ferns and mosses and rhododendrons. Leaving Palabadula, the air becomes decidedly more invigorating, and after crossing some padi fields we came to a feeder of the hundred-headed Kalu Ganga, 30 feet wide, spanned by a rustic wooden bridge, floored with little sticks an inch thick called *mopas*.

Half an hour's rough climbing lands us now at the foot of a grim overhanging cliff, where we halt once more and swallow a draught of tepid coffee at Ooda Pawanella, the highest inhabited hamlet on the mountain. Starting onwards again, we make the best progress we can through the dry boulder-strewn bed of a torrent, along which lie scattered in chaotic confusion the interlacing roots of trees and stony *débris* of all shapes and sizes. This heart-breaking and sole-cutting state of things lasts until we reach a height of 2700 feet, where the coolies halt us at the edge of a dizzy precipice, which I judged to be 700 or 800 feet in depth, down which a young girl named Nilihela once dashed herself for love's sake. The place is noteworthy for a fine double echo, which, on the girl's name being called aloud, gives it back in tones which the natives regard with awe, as the answering spirit of the unfortunate maiden. At this part of the road we pass at intervals little rough wooden resting-places, with here and there a cairn, upon which each wayfarer scrupulously casts a stone for luck, and a projecting crag known as Ooroohota, or "the snout of the pig." Another rushing torrent, with a bridge of a single beam of wood, and then a couple of miles through dense forest, bring us to the little plateau of Diyabetma, or "division of the waters." We are here at the head-waters of the Kalu Ganga, and from this point the streams which we have hitherto seen flowing south are replaced by others which take a northerly or north-westerly direction as they hasten along to meet the Karu Ganga, whose cradle is hidden in the topmost clefts of the cloud-capped mountain. At Diyabetma there is an enchanting and magnificent prospect over leagues of rolling patanas[1] and jungle and virgin forest to the ranges beyond, with here and there the gleam of a white-stemmed areca palm. Turning from earth to heaven, I saw, for the first time since leaving the plains, the majestic "sugar-loaf" cone of the Peak, distant by the path 3 miles, towering in its solitary grandeur into the blue, with the little temple of the Sri-pada just visible on the top. The sight of the whole mass as seen from this point put me in mind of the view of Monte Viso, rising in the west as you descend from the Alps into Turin.

It needed some exercise of courage to turn my eyes from such a view, and to tramp onwards towards cloudland; but if the climb seemed to get harder with every step and stumble, we rose each moment face to face with fresh objects of beauty and interest. At last we are at Sitaganga, or Sitagangelle, on holy ground. This is not only the place of purification for every pilgrim, but also

[1] The savannahs of Ceylon.

the abode of Sita, wife of Rama, who has been the *dewa* of the stream ever since the far-off days when here she lay as a captive and here she bathed, thereby making the water, as she has made many streams in India, an object of veneration to all ages. The torrent roars and blusters along a bed of the wildest nature, shadowed by trees and flanked by steep cliffs. In the glassy pools, at the foot of a cluster of huge boulders, pilgrims may at all times be seen performing their ceremonial ablutions, without which any farther ascent is a mere waste of labour. At the season of the annual pilgrimage the scene must be a striking one, when the pilgrims from all parts of Asia are gathered together, and either stand splashing in the water, or make their devotions to Sita, or rest upon the grassy margin chattering, or eating rice, or chewing the everlasting betel, while their many-coloured garments lie drying in the sun. Not far off is a rock called Diwiya-galla, on which is carved something which my "boy" assured me was a tiger's pad, but which in my infidel eyes bore as little resemblance to a feline foot as did its weird legend to a page of Macaulay. Half a mile above Sitaganga lies a small glen with steep banks, down which rough wooden ladders here and there facilitated our progress. On the far side, one of the nastiest places of the whole climb, a vast stretch of perfectly smooth and bare rock, is made a little easier by 200 steps cut in four flights, of which the last and highest, numbering ninety, is the best and most regular. These steps are said to have been cut by a potentate whose lineaments and autograph are roughly carved close by, and are declared by Buddhists to be (like the stones on Salisbury Plain) beyond the reach of accurate reckoning by ordinary mortals.

Now, as we are nearing at last the goal of our weary pilgrimage, we find ourselves face to face with the sorest trouble of all. From the time of leaving this rocky staircase to the moment of landing, blown and breathless, on the summit of the Peak, the pilgrim may be said literally to live with his life in his hand. Possibly a seasoned Alpine Club man might not think much of the perils to be encountered ; but I cannot help thinking that to ordinarily fashioned travellers, whose physical training has not soared to the higher branches of gymnastics, there is something deterrent in the idea of hanging on the bare rough face of a white-hot mountain 7000 feet above the sea, with one foot stuck hopelessly in the ill-shaped link of a rusty iron chain, of which the upper end only is made fast to the rock, and the rest sways merrily at its own sweet will beneath your weight to the rhythm of "a' the airts" of heaven; your other foot meanwhile seeking in an agonised forlorn way that missing link which you dare not look down to secure. Above, as you cling despairingly and long vainly for a prehensile tail or eyelid, there soars the pitiless peak to which you aspire; beneath there is nothing to speak of till you reach the bottom—somewhere. Still I was thankful enough at the moment for any kind of support, and I could have been fairly comfortable remembering how many had sought pardon for their sins by the same way before me, if only I could have driven from my head the ghastly thought, "Suppose that rusty old link up there comes away! it's bound to come some day: why not now?" And then I tried to realise how I should feel if I were picked up in little pieces 1000 feet below, and how little there would be to identify an Englishman, unknown to fame, in a suit of whites.

As I reached a level spot about thrice the size of this page, scarcely venturing to cast a look downwards, I asked my coolie in mild and gasping tones whether accidents ever happened at such places, and what would happen if a High Church Brahman and a Low Church Shintoist were to meet on the same chain, one going up and the other coming down? Of the latter situation he could frame no solution, but as to my other query he assured me, with the lightsome laugh of his race, that very seldom did anybody "come to grief." I have been told, however, that fatalities are more common than is supposed; the loss of a pilgrim or two not being an event likely to be noised abroad or marvelled at. A much more real marvel is how those chains ever came there. The bare idea is bewildering of anything but a mussel sticking up there, and making fast those huge rings on the face of the living rock. I confess I give it up, and can only express my regret that, for the sake of future pilgrims, the beneficent genius, be he hero or deity, who so far accomplished his good work did not complete it by securing the lower ends, or at least attaching them to a rail. As they are, they do but lie along and rest on the rocks, and are, moreover, clumsily made, with no two consecutive links alike. Regarding the origin of them we know nothing more trustworthy than the romance of Ashreef, who tells us that we owe them to Alexander the Great, who added to his other benefactions to mankind by "fixing chains with rings and rivets of brass and iron, the remains of which exist to this day, so that travellers by their assistance are enabled to climb the mountain of Serendib, and obtain glory by finding the sepulchre of Adam, on whom be the blessing of Allah!"

With which pious aspiration on behalf of the first gentleman of his day, I scramble with one final effort on to the topmost plateau, and, at the respectable height of 7700 feet above the sea, narrowly escape destruction in the moment of victory, by the mode in which I alight from the top of the last chain on to a most awkward corner of the summit. So bad, indeed, is the approach to this sacred eyrie that the first thing most pilgrims do is to fall head first forwards, which may be taken, as I sincerely trust it was in my own case, as a long-prepared and well-studied *salaam* to the *genius loci.* I may mention that the last chain of all at the top is known as "the chain of the creed," because of the involuntary expression of faith (in my case a shortened minatory form) which passes the lips of the pilgrim as he looks his last at the yawning abyss below, and sets his foot or his forehead, as the case may be, on level ground once more.

The top of the Peak is an elliptic area, within a wall 5 feet high, measuring some 80 feet from east to west, with the granite apex rising in the centre to a height of 10 feet and a circuit of 120. On the top of this central rock is an indented excavation some 6 feet long by 2½ wide, the Sri-pada in which the glowing imagination of the Buddhist discerns the outline of the foot of Gautama. It looks for all the world like the impression of a seal on wax, and bears but small resemblance to a human foot, owing in part to a depredation committed by some Chinese who, according to Ibn Batista, cut out the two biggest toes and deposited them in their own city of Tschu-thoung. At the time of the great pilgrimage this footprint is made into something more like what it professes to be, by means of the addition of a shabby brass frame studded with gems, looking not unlike bits of coloured glass, which the priest fits into a plaster moulding tinted like the true rock round it. There is little doubt that the excavation is partly natural, and equally little that the small elevated divisions representing the interstices of the toes are the work of man, inasmuch as they are of a different substance from the granite. Over the Sri-pada is a small open wooden temple, called "the gold-covered house," measuring 12 feet by 10, and held in its place by four iron chains, with a tiled canopy supported at each corner by low pillars connected by woodwork carved all over with the initials of pilgrims. At the time of the festival the roof of this Swiss-cottage-looking edifice is hung with white or coloured drapery, and flowers are scattered around.

The pilgrims, on reaching the end of their long climb, first make their prostrations before the shrine of Samana, 3 feet high, just below the Sri-pada, and then proceed to a bell fixed to a stone laid across two upright ones. The clapper attached to a leathern rope is pulled by each pilgrim, who thus ascertains whether he has on his way up duly performed his ablutions in the

Sitaganga. If all is right, the bell gives forth a wheezy sound, anything but reassuring in character; but if not, it refuses to speak, and the worshipper is disqualified from any further devotions until he has made up for his neglect. At the new year's gathering, or Awooroo-du-mangallc, pilgrims flock to the Peak in bands of 400 or 500 at a time, and when the above rites have been duly discharged, kneel and kiss the base of the central rock. At the same time their offerings of copper coins or cloth, gay rhododendrons or sweet champac bloom, or the unburst flower spathes of the areca palm, or perhaps merely a betel leaf or two, are laid just in front of the toes of the Sri-pada; while those who bring more substantial oblations of gold or jewels are allowed to climb the ten rough blocks of stone that lead to the temple itself, there to lay their gifts within the actual footprint, whence they are promptly swept by an acolyte, on their way to the private treasury of the priest. Then a religious service is held. A yellow-robed priest takes his stand on the rock close to the Sri-pada, with his face to the worshippers, who, ranged beneath, kneel with high uplifted hands joined palm to palm. In a loud clear voice the priest sentence by sentence recites certain articles of faith and the roll of religious duties, to which the people make their responses. Frequent shouts of *Sadhoo*[1] are raised, and then all present fall to promiscuous embracing and salutation. An old gray-haired woman (how in the name of fortune did she ever find her way to the top?) makes her *salaam* to an equally venerable-looking man, whose feet she kisses as she kneels before him. He raises her up, and then the old couple stand side by side to receive the *salaams* of the younger folk. These in their turn are salaamed by the still more juvenile, after which all hob and nob together, and exchange betel leaves, by way of confirming the ties of kinship, consolidating family affection, and obliterating animosities. Then all gather again round the central stone and receive the sacerdotal benediction; the cracked bell is tinkled, a draught swallowed by each from a little spring on the north side, which is supposed to communicate directly with Paradise, and all descend once more to the (by comparison) lower regions, there, we

[1] *Sadhoo* really means "well done! good!" and may be taken as equivalent to the "hallelujah" of revival meetings.

will hope, to lead for the future better and more virtuous lives.[1]

I once passed a night on the neighbouring and somewhat higher mountain of Pedrutallagalla, and may give my experiences as applying with equal truth to Adam's Peak. No sooner had the last embers of our little fire grown dim and I had fallen asleep, than I was roused by the chill blasts of wind laden with moisture, which whistled and sang through the crannies of the little hut in which we had taken up our quarters. So cold did it become that I rose and went outside, and spent the night in tramping up and down to keep myself warm. True I was somewhere about 5° north latitude, but I was also 8000 feet above the sea. Though for a while my eyelids were heavy with slumber, I can never regret that I remained out in the open, for I was more than repaid by the wonderful scenes I witnessed in cloudland. It was nearly full moon, and by her light I could see the crests of the surrounding mountains with great distinctness, while in every nearer cleft and gully below lay impenetrable shadows that made them look

[1] Note L.

as of depth unfathomable. Masses of pearly gray mist floated hither and thither in fantastic shapes, from which now and again a fragment of cloud would detach itself and stream away on a voyage of discovery on its own account. Then borne along by the restless night airs cloudy battalions would come sweeping past, breaking themselves in feathery foam against the battlements of the steep mountain barriers. It required no great amount of credulity to accept the belief of the simple coolie who lay snoring at my feet, and to discern in those shifting forms of vapour the visible expression of the existence of spirit guardians, who for ages unnumbered had haunted their native fastnesses. As morning came on apace the wind fell, and the first level sunbeams from over the Kandyan hills lit up what looked like a glassy expanse of water, the colour of the down on a cygnet's breast, studded with countless wooded islands; a deception of nature, which without the aid of memory it was difficult to conceive of as a mere fanciful creation, until beneath the gathering power of the thirsty sun-god mist and shadow and cloud had rolled away, and beneath me there lay once more the firm outlines of rock and wood and mountain.

I cannot attempt to give an idea of the grandeur of the view from the top of Adam's Peak, which in some respects is not unlike that from the top of Monte Rotondo in Corsica, although to my mind incomparably finer. On every side

Majestic woods, of every vigorous green,
Stage above stage, high waving o'er the hills,
Or to the far horizon wide diffused—
A boundless deep immensity of shade.

To the north and east rise the soft outlines of the Kandyan range; south and west is a rolling sea of verdure, with many a fantastic crag and yawning ravine and flashing cataract: the river whose babbling at this great height is hushed seems to wind almost at your feet; while far away over many a mile of plain and jungle the eye can catch

The sunlit silver of the sounding surf,

as it breaks on the palm-fringed shore of ocean. In truth it is

A land of wonders, which the sun still eyes
With ray direct, as of the lovely realm
Enamour'd, and delighting there to dwell.

Well does Sir Emerson Tennent write: "The panorama is perhaps the grandest in the world, as no other mountain, although surpassing it in altitude, presents the same unobstructed view over land and sea. Around it to the north and east the traveller looks down on the zone of lofty hills that encircle the Kandyan kingdom, whilst to the westward the eye is carried far over undulating plains threaded by rivers like cords of silver, till in the purple distance the glitter of the sunbeams on the sea marks the line of the Indian Ocean."

And so,

As the sweet day
With drooping lids lies dying,

I descend amid the lengthening shadows with questionings in my heart. Whence comes it that hundreds of millions of my fellow-men, many of them better and wiser than I, regard this place whereon I have been standing with as much reverence as the devout Catholic regards that little landing at the head of the Scala Santa? The mere fact that on its summit up there in cloudland there is the impress of a human foot has little to do with the answer which I crave.

To me the clustered legends are but as so many after-thoughts. What I want to know is *how* did the Mohammedan and the Buddhist and the Brahman ever come at the beginning to look upon that hollow in the rock as a footprint? And I would ask, Where else upon earth is there such a religious service ever held? It may be an easy thing for the clever young man who has succeeded in solving the insoluble to treat the whole cult as a jest, and, in the spirit of Mr. Wackford Squeers, to call it "a rum and a holy thing"; but we may not forget that the dissensions of Christianity are unknown to these simple folk, who, though of different races and varying forms of creed, kneel side by side in the presence of that which is for them the most sacred thing on earth. For my own part, I deem them to be above both our protest and our pity.

No one whose heart is in tune with Nature can stand on this "throne of clouds" and look out upon one of the most sublime scenes of earth, without acknowledging the subtle power of a mysterious and beneficent influence. A St. Paul's Cathedral may fall a victim to the flames. The dome of St. Peter's may be shattered at any moment. As each sun rises and sets, so surely do each and all of man's most massive fanes tend to their decay. But here, on this lonely mountain peak, in this temple not made with hands, above the clang and clamour of the nations, we know that our feet stand in the unchanging presence-chamber of an eternal and omnipotent Spirit:

> *Spared and blest by time;*
> *Looking tranquillity, while man plods*
> *His way through thorns to ashes.*

CHAPTER VII

FAUNA

Without adhering strictly to proper zoological order, the place of honour among the Ceylon fauna belongs without doubt to that "great masterpiece of nature" the Elephant. It was long a matter of belief, and I have seen it stated in more than one popular work upon natural history, that there are but two species of elephant upon earth—the Asiatic or Indian, and the African. The observations of Temminck, Tennent, and others have, however, shown that this is an erroneous idea, and that there is a third equally distinct, and known as *Elephas Sumatranus,* found in the island of Sumatra. It has been placed beyond a doubt by Professor Schlegel that with this last species the Ceylon elephant is identical.

The points of difference between the African and Indian kinds are well known. The former is considerably the larger beast, and has the highest point at the shoulder, with a hollow back, enormous ears, and a convex forehead. The Indian (*Elephas Indicus*), on the other hand, is not only smaller but has a convex back, the lowest point at the shoulder, small ears, and concave forehead. Between him and his Sumatran or Singhalese brother there are several points of difference, seeing that he has a stouter and more powerful frame and a longer and more slender proboscis, the end of which is flatter and covered with a coarser hair. "It is indeed," says Tennent, "a singular illustration of geographical distribution that two remote islands should possess in common a species unknown in any other quarter of the globe."

As a rule the Ceylon elephant, called by the Singhalese *gadjah*, has no tusks, but in their place a pair of grubbers or "tushes," about 12 inches long and 2 inches thick, set in the upper jaw. Sir Samuel Baker has recorded that he once saw a male tusker with 6-foot tusks, but such are exceedingly rare. In Africa and India both sexes have tusks, although those in the female are rather the smaller. In Ceylon the elephant uses his "tushes" to grub up the earth with, to strip off the bark of trees, and to snap boughs and creepers. According to a theory more ingenious than sound, he has no need of tusks, owing to the profusion of rivers and waterholes all round him; whereas his namesake in other lands could not do without them, seeing that they are his only instruments for digging wells in the sand, and for getting up the juicy roots of the succulent plants with which he quenches his thirst.

The Singhalese in asserting that the elephant lives for 300 years go beyond the truth, its average age being not more than 70.[1] It is a fact that the carcase of an elephant dead from natural causes is seldom found. Some say, as the Greeks of old said, that the dead giant is buried by his comrades. There is a certain place near Anuradhapoora to which it is said (in agreement with Sinbad's adventure) that all elephants come when they feel death approaching. This recalls an observation which Darwin made to the same effect regarding the llamas in Patagonia.

The elephant in the lowlands of Ceylon is of much value as a field labourer. He will draw a

[1] Note M.

harrow, with a second one attached, and a roller behind, thus performing three operations at the same time. Indeed there are few things he cannot do in the way of work. In the construction of dams and bridges his skill is well known. He is able to move with the utmost ease beams of heavy wood 20 feet long, which he will place exactly in position without assistance, rolling them over with his head and feet alternately. He is, however, an expensive labourer, his ordinary daily food consisting of 600 pounds of green fodder, 15 pounds of flour made up into large scones, a pound of ghee or buffalo butter, together with a quantity of salt and jagery or palm sugar, the whole costing about seven shillings.

Elephant-shooting is strictly regulated by law, and there is a royalty of 100 rupees payable upon each animal exported, in addition to which a permit must be produced from the district where he was captured. Notwithstanding his huge bulk the animal is a bit of a coward, whose natural timidity is increased rather than lessened by domestication. It is difficult in India to buy one that will calmly stand the attack of a wild animal, even the best being apt to swerve sometimes to one side as a tiger makes his spring. But the "rogue"—*hora allia*, as the Singhalese call him —no less than the "must" elephant, is a most dangerous and reckless beast.

The Singhalese are in the habit of measuring an elephant's height from the diameter of his footprint or spoor, which they multiply by six.

I quote the following interesting instance of elephantine instinct from Sir Samuel Baker's pages. At a certain place in the south of Ceylon there are large numbers of Bhel trees (*Æglé marmelos*), with hard-shelled brown fruit like a cricket ball, highly aromatic and sweet. When quite ripe this fruit is the favourite food of elephants, who flock thither in great numbers from all parts every year just at the exact time when it reaches maturity.

A story of a different kind serves to show the pachyderm's vitality. Major Skinner, the great Ceylon roadmaker, and Mr. Forbes, once when out shooting together put several bullets into an elephant, which after staggering for a few yards dropped as if dead. They proceeded, according to custom, to cut off the tail as a trophy, and then started off in pursuit of the rest of the herd.

They had not gone far, when a beater came running after them to tell them that the animal had revived and killed a coolie. They promptly returned, and made sure of their work by firing several more shots into the creature's carcase, after which they held an inquest upon the remains of his unfortunate victim, at the same time giving orders for the digging of a grave. Just as they were sealing up the evidence to forward it to Government, the coolie upon whom they had "sat," followed the elephant's example and came to life again! Strange to say, the man, like the beast, again collapsed, both ultimately expiring after some hours.

The only other pachyderm found in the island is a less formidable but sufficiently mischievous member of the *Sus* genus, the Boar, called by the Singhalese *waloora*. Is there any country on earth where the pig does not flourish? In a domesticated state he is found in many different varieties of breed, but wild he is very much the same all the world over. Ceylon, which possesses the largest and most ferocious boar (*Sus scropha*, or *barbatus*), must be a perfect paradise for him, with its abundant food all the year round, its plentiful water-supply, its roots, snakes, and dead animals always at hand to satisfy the cravings of the porker. It is not an unusual thing for a Ceylon boar to scale at six hundredweight. It is greedily eaten by the natives, but Europeans do not fancy it on account of its exceedingly eclectic tastes in the matter of food. The animal when chased can outstrip the best horse; there is no superfluous fat on him in his native wilds.

Although classed among the Carnivora, it is really doubtful whether the structurally omnivorous Sloth Bear (*Prochilus labiatus*) or *oosa* ever touches flesh. As the only representative in Ceylon of the Ursidæ family, it has a black coat, worthless as fur, and is quite the most vicious variety of Indian bears. It has been known to attack even men and elephants without provocation. Its favourite food is roots, honey, termites, grubs, and ants; and it lives, not as in other lands among the mountains, but in the ravines and rocky fastnesses of the hot plains, or in the hollow stumps of old trees, whence at night it sallies forth in search of food. There is no animal more dreaded by the Singhalese, who often carry a *kodeli* or light axe in self-defence,—not without good reason, as it is no uncommon thing to see their faces badly gashed by the bear's claws, which are 2 inches long. The flesh is excellent although a little coarse, and its fat cannot be surpassed as a lubricant, keeping good in the hottest weather if properly sealed up closely in a bottle and exposed to the sun, as is done with tiger's fat in India.

More common and less dreaded is the Chetah, native *cooteah*, which in Ceylon is a different animal from the native leopard, with which it is often wrongly classed. Both in habits and appearance it is quite distinct, in that it is smaller, and possesses (according to some observers) no retractile power in its claws, which are not curved but formed like the toe-nails of a dog. These claws, from being used in the mangling of decomposed carcases, sometimes inflict dangerous wounds, gangrene being induced by inoculation. The chetah is usually about 3 feet high at the shoulder, and 6 feet long from nose to tip, with round black spots the size of a shilling.

The more rare leopard (*Felis pardus*), really the true panther, is from 7 to 8 feet in length, and has spots only on the legs, the back and sides being covered with black rings with a brown centre. The leopard is fond of making war upon monkeys, which are immensely afraid of it, and are said finally to succumb to the powerful fascination of its eye. One very rare variety (*Felis melas*) is black-coated, with spots that can only be seen in certain lights. In Ceylon all these animals are, as I have said, commonly called chetahs, and they must not be confounded with the hunting chetah (*chitah*) of India, not a pure feline but lanky and long-legged, unable to climb trees, and usually considered as a link between felines and canines. All are destructive enemies of live stock, refusing nothing from a cow to a chicken. A common mode of destroying them is by fastening a line to a gun set near a bait so placed that the trigger is pulled directly the animal approaches. Among the hills chetahs are caught in a trap made by supporting the half-fallen trunk of a tree in such a way that it falls just as the animal passes beneath to seize the bait. This device, like all other wild animal traps in Ceylon, is not devoid of danger to the unwary traveller.

One night during my stay in a hill bungalow we heard a great commotion going on in the cow-house at some little distance. In the morning the thatched roof was found torn through, and inside was a chetah lying dead, with the horn of a dead cow right through its body. Beside the combatants stood a calf, which had been the object of attraction to the marauder. Sir Emerson Tennent has recorded a precisely similar incident. As a rule the chetah is a coward, and it is only when pressed by famine that it will attack a homestead. Dogs often fall victims to it; many a one that would be more than a match in a fair fight being killed by the animal's sudden spring on to the back of its neck.

The Canidæ in Ceylon consist largely of crowds of miserable mangy pariahs that infest the streets of the towns. In Buddhist literature and native ditties the Jackal (*Canis aureus*) figures as a member of the habitual criminal class, the type of low cunning, with a reputation not inferior to that of Master Reynard in the shires. He gets his name from the Arabic *chathal*, and is called in Ceylon *nareeah* or *kholah*. He is the incarnation of famishing despair, and an incorrigible marauder in the matter of pigs, lambs, and poultry, and has been known to filch puppies when lying with their mother. Nor has the creature any objection to cooked meat when he can get it, and, moreover, will devour anything from an old shoe to an oil-rag. Although he stinks badly the natives sometimes eat him. He is as big as a good-sized fox, but with less of a "brush." There are large packs of jackals on the lowlands, where they often pull down deer. In the matter of noise this beast can give points to any of his fellow-denizens or to the dingo (*warrigal*) of Australia. His nocturnal musings, combined with the airy attentions of the mosquito, are more than enough to banish sleep and encourage unparliamentary language. There is a world of sharp complaining in his cry. It is as if the portals of a hotter place than Ceylon had been thrown open, and a trumpet put into the hand of each liberated fiend, with strict orders to blow *fortissimo*. The common cat on the war-path at home has undeniable power, but he or she can never hope to reach the top notes of the jackal. Confining himself mainly to one tune, he begins at a low pitch in a semi-apologetic manner; soon he rises a little, still with a suspicion of explanation that he never meant to make quite so much noise, but that it has by this time passed beyond his control. Then finally the flood-gates of song are thrown open, and as if to say that now he cares for nobody, he parts the night air with yells of ecstatic *abandon.*

To the smaller feline carnivora belongs the family of Viverridæ, including the glossy Civet Cat or *genette* (*V. Indica*), the native *ooralawa,* 3 feet long, with gray black-spotted fur and ringed tail, a most destructive creature among poultry. Under its tail is an offensive gland which secretes musk worth six shillings a pound. When alive the genette smells horribly, but after death the secretion forms the well-known perfume, which is obtained also from the musk-deer, musk-ox, musk-rat, and musk-beetle.

Closely connected is the Palm Cat (*Paradoxurus typus*) or Puzzle-tail, called by the Singhalese *oogoodora,* that sleeps all day in the palm heads, and prowls at night round the hen-roost. Another viverra is the Ichneumon (from a Greek word meaning a "tracker") or Mongoos, of which there are four genera. *Herpestes vitticollis,* the Singhalese *loco moogata,* is known also as the Ceylon badger or Streaked mongoos; it has a bushy fur coat, and is found chiefly round Jaffna and Trincomalee. *Herpestes nyula* is beautifully marked in a zigzag pattern all over the body and head, and while smaller than the Egyptian variety, which of old received divine honours, is no less clean and nimble. The gray or common mongoos (*H. griseus*), 3 feet long, with wiry coat and curved claws, has a great liking for snakes, for which reason it is never killed by the natives. There is a common idea that this animal when bitten averts certain death by feeding upon a bitter prophylactic plant (*Ophiorhiza mongoos*) which the natives call *katteya*. This is, however, more than doubtful, the truth seeming to be that it is constitutionally poison-proof, of which it is not the only instance in the animal world. It is well known that the hedgehog (*Erinaceus Europæus*) is impervious to the effects of prussic acid, arsenic, and other deadly poisons, and enjoys a hearty meal of cantharides. The extreme activity of the mongoos usually enables it to avoid the spring of the snake and to fasten its fangs at the back of the reptile's head, where it clings until the spine is broken.

Another ichneumon (*H. fulvescens*), of a bright orange colour, is found only in Ceylon.

Quadrumana are answerable for a great deal of

noise in the country parts of Ceylon. There are five genera of *Simiadæ*, four of which are Wanderoos, each inhabiting a different district, and the fifth the Rilawa. The latter (*Macacus pileatus*), called by the natives *munga*, is a brown or olive-gray bonneted macaque with a smooth pale face, capable of the funniest grimaces, and a tuft of hair upon the top of its head. The Tamuls teach it to dance and smoke, and dress it up in grotesque costumes. It is a good-tempered little creature, but should it happen to be crossed knows how to make excellent use of its teeth. Robert Knox says concerning it that "it does a deal of mischief to the corn and fruit," whereas the wanderoo "does but little mischief, keeping in the woods, eating only leaves and buds of trees." This last-named animal is *Presbytes ursinus*, called by the Singhalese *ooandoora*, a word merely meaning "monkey." According to some, it is a species of macaque, but more probably others are right in considering it a link between the macaque and the baboon. In India it is known as *neel bhunder*, black monkey. It keeps closely to the upland forests and is rarely seen by Europeans. But at daybreak I have heard its peculiar cry of *how! how!*

P. cephalopterus is the wanderoo of the low country, sometimes known as *Leucoprymnus Nestor*, a black brown-eyed creature with a snow-white beard and a tufted tail. It is smaller than *P. ursinus* and more active, but does not equal the rilawa for mischief. When captured it becomes melancholy, but makes a good pet, and is most cleanly in its ways, for a monkey. There are many of these wanderoos round Damboola in the north. On my way to Anuradhapoora I now and then saw troops of them and of rilâwas overhead, swinging from bough to bough with almost lightning speed, often with their young clinging to their bodies. *P. Thersites*, a black variety, is found but rarely; *P. Priamus*, gray, and the largest of all, lives in the hills round Jaffna. White wanderoos are sometimes seen near Damboola. The average height is from 3 to 4 feet, the weight 80 pounds. From the fact that in this species both upper and lower jaws are in a straight line with the forehead, it has a very human appearance, more so, indeed, than any other simian of the East. I may here mention the popular belief in Ceylon and India that he who sees a dead monkey, a straight coconut palm, or a padi bird's nest, will live for ever.

The Lemuridæ are represented by the small brown and black Loris (*L. gracilis*), or Ceylon sloth (Tamul *thavangu*), peculiar to the island and the Asiatic archipelago. I have seen these creatures coiled up fast asleep sitting upon their heads, which were hidden away between the legs. The muzzle is long, sharp, and turned up; the eyes very large, the limbs slender and delicate, the body 9 inches long, of a gray rusty tinge, whiter underneath, with a tail conspicuous by its absence. At night the eyes of the loris shine like phosphorescent fire, as it creeps with perfect noiselessness along a branch to dart its paw upon a sleeping bird.

Among the Cheiroptera, or wing-handed family, we are first attracted by a creature strange to English eyes, the Roussette (*Pteropus rubricollis* or *Edwardsii*), known to the Singhalese as the *loco voulha*, but familiar to us as the Flying Fox, a name derived from its very foxy head. This animal has but twenty-four vertebræ—fewer than any other creature. The bones of the fore-limbs are elongated, and support a large membrane by the help of which it is popularly said to fly. The thumb-joint is furnished with a nail; the hind feet are small and armed with sharp claws. The roussette is about a foot long and has a wing-spread of 3 or 4 feet; it feeds upon eggs and insects, and is a great devourer of the guava, banana, fig, and other fruits, as well as of the buds of the silk-cotton tree. When "flying" its young one often clings to its breast or sides. When laid upon the ground it is perfectly helpless, having no limbs capable of progressive movement; when asleep it hangs by one foot, with its head wrapped in the folds of its "wings." The flesh is said to taste like hare, and I am sorry to be obliged to add that the creature occasionally gets very drunk upon palm toddy. It is found here and there in very large numbers, and is as great a pest here as in Australia, where it has provoked active measures for its extermination. During last year a party of scientific gentlemen made an experiment in New South Wales to ascertain the possibility of destroying the flying foxes wholesale by dynamite, but the method was found impracticable, and the flying-fox still flourishes, to the great detriment of the fruit crops.

Bats are in large numbers, swarming at sunset round every dwelling, and thronging roofs and ruins. Many persons do not know that under a microscope the hair of a bat looks just like the common "mare's-tail" plant, being covered with minute scales, all variously arranged round a central shaft. There are in Ceylon sixteen species of bats, of which *Hipposideros aureus* is yellow, and *Rhinolophus rubidus* a ruddy brown. Its relative *R. affinis*, or horse-shoe-headed bat, is (like the British *R. ferrum-equinum*) a strange-looking creature, with a substance like a leaf growing upright upon the end of its nose. The prettiest of all is a tiny species, *Scotophilus Coromandelicus*, no bigger than a bumble-bee, shiny black, and very tame and trusting. I have caught one at Galle Face by merely putting a tumbler over it.

Of the Talpidæ, or Mole family, several genera are found, of which the chief is the Sorex or shrew, with long sharp muzzle, small eyes, broad ears, and short tail. *S. montanus*, *S. ferrugineus*, and *Feroculus macropus* are none of them less pugnacious than their English kinsfolk: combats take place between them which in larger animals would be terrific, but with these tiny creatures are only ludicrous. *S. murinus* is the Musk-rat, called by the natives *soudeli*, like a shrew but larger.

First place in the order Ungulata must be awarded to the imposing Buffalo (*Bubalus buffelus*), called by the Singhalese *mee-harak*, a powerful, morose, and vicious brute, plentiful everywhere, and the shooting of which affords sport not unattended by danger. In some districts buffaloes are tamed and made to work in the rice-fields, or to draw the heavy salt carts, but they are never to be trifled with. Their smooth horns are, like those of all horned animals in the island, shorter than in other countries, owing possibly to a deficiency in the pasturage of such lime and phosphates as are necessary for the growth of horn. Buffaloes in the pleasures of rumination sometimes wallow so deeply in the watery mud that they stick inextricably, and are then an easy prey. All you can see of them is the eyes and muzzle, the horns being under the surface.

With limbs as graceful as those of a deer the little ox or Zebu (*Bos Indicus*), called by the natives *harakah*, draws along with his mate the *bhandy* or two-wheeled cart thatched with plaited coco-nut leaves. A crossbar at the end of a pole rests on the neck in front of the hump, against which the animal pushes, the bar being kept from slipping upwards by a rope which passes through holes and round the throat. They are pretty, dark, slim-necked creatures, with a hump and a long silky dewlap, and are the common beasts of draught. Oxen are largely used for ploughing and trampling the mud on the padi fields, and at harvest time for treading out the grain. They are, unfortunately, from time to time subject to the deadly ravages of a feverish influenza or murrain, by which thousands perish.

Among the Cervine tribe the largest species is the *Sambhur* (*Rusa Aristotelis*), the native *sona russa*, the Great Axis of Cuvier, often but erroneously called an elk. In height it exceeds every other species in the world except the Wapiti and the Moose, standing usually 5 feet at the shoulder, with a weight of 500 or 600 pounds. It makes excellent venison, especially when it has had opportunities of feeding upon its favourite food, the young leaf of the cinchona. This savage and morose animal is sooty-brown in colour, with patches of tan over the eyes, tail, and feet. The male has a full dark mane, with antlers set upon a long footstalk. Sambhur are seldom shot, but give first-rate sport to hounds, for which purpose the best strain of English foxhounds has proved a failure. Far better runs are made with dogs crossed either between foxhound and pointer, mastiff and bloodhound, or greyhound and kangaroo dog. It is a grand sight to see a sambhur of 600 pounds' weight dashing for his life down a steep broken hill at a headlong pace. Another kind, the Spotted deer (*Axis maculata*), native *chetool*, the only gregarious deer in Ceylon, is found in large herds in the north, and is perhaps the prettiest and most graceful of all the race. It is a dark reddish brown, with satin-like coat dashed with snowy spots, proud head, lovely black eyes, and body rather larger than a fallow. The antlers, shorter than in India, are gracefully curved, thin, and very sharp. The chetool is rarely to be seen between sunrise and sunset, and when chased has a turn of speed surpassing, on good ground, the swiftest greyhound.

The Barking deer (*Stylocerus*, or *cervus*, *Muntjac*) is a small elegant animal, but is excelled in beauty by the tiny hornless Mouse, Musk, or

Moose deer (*Moschus meminna*), with spotted gray coat and rat-like head. It is called by the Singhalese *walmeniya*, its scientific name being a corruption of the Dutch *muis* or mouse. It is but 2 feet long and the same in height or less, and in its movements among the rocks is marvellously agile. It has two small tusks with which it digs up bulbs. "Here," says Robert Knox, "is a creature no bigger than a hare, though every part rightly resembles a deer, of a gray colour with white spots, and good meat." I may mention that when the British troops entered Kandy in 1803 they found in the palace five beautiful milk-white deer, which were looked upon as great curiosities.

The Red deer is very common and quite different from its Scottish cousin (*Cervus elaphus*), measuring only from 2 to 3 feet at the shoulder, and with horns but 8 inches long. The carcase, weighing 50 pounds, is out of all proportion to the size of the legs, which, however, can carry it along with amazing speed. A deer peculiar to Ceylon is *C. orizus*, almost as large as the sambhur, but with a different arrangement of spots on the coat.

Passing on to the order Rodentia, I must name

first the clumsy Porcupine (*Hystrix cristata, H. leucura*), common enough, but rarely seen on account of its shy nature. It is a destructive animal among the cocos, and crafty in avoiding snares. The easiest way to get at it is by smoking it out of its burrow. The flesh is considered a delicacy.

In the family of Jerboidæ, two species of Squirrel (Singhalese *rookaali*) peculiar to Ceylon are found, one of which is the Palm squirrel (*Sciurus penicillatus*). In the sub-genus *S. Layardi* (native *egala dandoleyna*), as in the Flying squirrel (*Pteromys petaurista*), and the Colugo of Java, the skin of the flank is developed into a parachute-like expansion, as thin as note-paper, affixed to the fore and hind limbs, by means of which it does *not* fly, but takes huge leaps in mid-air buoyed up by the distended skin. On the hind feet are five toes armed with claws. Its chief enemies are the civet cat and the tree snakes.

Another rodent is the Bandicoot (*Mus bandicota*) which gets its name from the Tamul *pandi-koku* or pig-rat. It is 2 feet long, weighs 3 or 4 pounds, and has a long pointed nose, with which it digs up and destroys whole rows of the sweet potato. In general appearance it may be likened to a rat the size of a cat ; it is a clean herbivorous feeder, and when killed tastes like young pork.

Last, although foremost in all works of mischief, is the Rat proper, fast becoming a veritable plague. The Coffee-rat (*Golunda Elliotti*), a variety of the South Indian rat (*Mus hirsutus*), is, like the lemming of Norway (*Myodes lemmus* or *Mus decumanus*) and the *musang* of Java, a terribly destructive pest. Curious to relate, the coffee cherries pass through the animal's body undigested, and are collected and used as food by the natives. At Oovah and in other parts rats are cut open by the Veddahs, smoke-dried, fried in coco-nut oil, and eaten, unfortunately not in such numbers as to lead to any hope of their being kept under by such means. A rat (*Mus Zeylanicus*) peculiar to the island is found in large numbers in the Cinnamon Gardens at Colombo.

The only individual of the toothless Edentata belongs to the Manina group, and is known as the Great Scaled Ant-eater (*Manis crassicaudata*), called by the Singhalese *caballaya*, or Negombo devil, but known in India as the Bujjerkeet, and allied to the larger species of Africa known as the Phattagin. It has a thick body covered with sharp-edged horny overlapping scales, with here and there a brown bristle or two showing, and a most noisome odour. Its tail is flattened, its head small, with elongated muzzle, small ears and black eyes; the limbs are short, stout, and extremely powerful; on the fore feet are large claws, which when the creature walks bend back under the feet, so that in reality it treads upon the knuckles or roots of the claws. The hind feet are not unlike those of a land tortoise, oval, with cushion-like soles. The tongue can protrude 12 inches and is covered with a viscous saliva. This rare creature is called in Malaysia *Pangoelin*, a word derived from its habit of sleeping rolled up in a ball, with the sharp-pointed scales outwards, in which state it is impervious to attack. It is a slow-moving creature, and lives with its mate in recesses of the rocks, and produces two or three young each year. Cuvier's assertion as to its climbing powers has been doubted, but I can state as a fact that it does do so, in search of black ants, by means of its hooked feet and a peculiar oblique grasp of its tail. The *caballaya*, although detested by the natives, is perfectly harmless, and seems to enjoy being made a pet of; but its habits are dirty, and it is positively alive with parasites.

The last family of mammalia we shall find in the great Cetaceans of the waters that break upon the shores of Ceylon. The Spermaceti Whale (*C. macrocephalus*) or Cachalot, otherwise the oil-head (Italian *capidoglio*), is caught in large numbers off the coast. From the head is obtained the spermaceti, a liquid oily substance, which after exposure to the air becomes hardened and freed from oil, and is then purified by a treatment of potass and various meltings. From one whale are obtained 24 barrels of spermaceti and about 100 barrels of oil, while the intestines supply 40 or 50 pounds' weight of a morbid gray fatty secretion, the ambergris so much used in perfumery, worth 20 shillings an ounce. It is said that the ambergris always contains certain black spots, marks from the beaks of *Sepia octopodia*, which are the animal's favourite food.[1] When caught the whale is towed alongside and generally hoisted up to the rigging

[1] Note N.

out of the way of sharks. The head is cut off whole, and then begins the work of flensing, or cutting out the blubber with sharp spades, an operation which brings together the sharks and sea-birds in multitudes.

The Dugong (*Halicorë dugong*), of the sub-order Sirenia, is twin-brother to the lazy uncouth manatee of the Atlantic, and is found chiefly in the shallow water near Adam's Bridge, whither it is attracted by the vast quantities of marine algæ, which it tears up by the roots with its two large incisor teeth. It measures from 7 to 10 feet and tastes like veal. This animal belongs to a family whose grotesque resemblance to a human form, and attitude when carrying or suckling its young, gave rise to the fabled mermaid. Ælian peopled the Indian seas with cetaceans in the form of satyrs. Megasthenes records the existence of a creature in the sea like a bearded woman. At a later period both the Portuguese and the Dutch, and not a few of our own English mariners, firmly believed in *zee-menschen*, *zee-wyven*, and mer-maidens. Valentyn writing in 1727 says: "If any narrative in the world deserves credit it is this; since not only one but two mermen together were seen by so many eye-witnesses. Should the stubborn world, however, hesitate to believe it, it matters nothing; as there are people who would deny that such cities as Rome, Constantinople, or Cairo exist, merely because they themselves have not happened to see them." I cannot resist adding a reference to one mermaid, who is said by the same writer to have been caught and carried to Haarlem, where she was taught to spin, and where after a few years she died in the Christian faith.

Among the 325 species of BIRDS, of which 38 are peculiar to Ceylon, we cannot include many sweet songsters. Indeed from observation in many lands I am inclined to believe that a cold, or at least a temperate, climate is necessary for the production of song. While, however, in plumage the birds of Ceylon are less gaudy than those of India and America, and in variety of song less sweet-voiced than those of Europe, they excel all others in grace of form no less than in the rich melodious character of many of their calls. It must not be supposed that the feathered tribes are conspicuous by their silence either in the hills or plains. There is the oreole, with its charming flute-like note; the long-tailed thrush (*Kittacincla macrura*), not one whit inferior to its namesake nearer home; the soothing note of the dove, and the familiar song of the Nuwara Eliya robin (*Pratincola atrata*). Many other old English friends too are to be seen and heard: starlings, wagtails, wood-pigeons, owls, crows, hawks, kites, herons, and the ubiquitous sparrow as saucy as in a London square.

Most gaudy of all are the Pea-fowl (*Pavo cristatus*), not as we see them in England in ones and twos preening themselves sedately on the sunny lawn of a country house, but (at least in certain districts) in flocks of forty or fifty together, and behaving in the wildest and most abandoned manner. There is no more brilliant sight in the tropics than a cluster of these magnificent birds in their wild state spreading and drying their gorgeous trains in the sun, for which purpose they are fond of perching on the dead branches of trees. Alas! that so beautiful a creature should give utterance to such wailful sounds. At early dawn if near at hand they utterly banish sleep with their clamorous screams. As a set-off, however, I may add that, as they take a long time to rise in the air, they are easy to shoot; and, moreover, are excellent eaten hot, which is the best, as it is the last atonement they can make. Was not their flesh known in the old days of chivalry as "the food of lovers and the meat of lords"? The usual way of treating them is to cut the breast up into cutlets and to make the remains into a rich soup. When you have once tasted peacock soup you can forgive him anything.

Scarcely less gay in plumage is the graceful Bird of Paradise (*Tchitrea paradisi*), known as the "cotton-thief," because of the two long white or brown feathers in its tail. In the Philippines it is called "God's bird."

The Magpie-robin (*Copsychus saularis*), called by the natives the dayal-bird, sings beautifully at sunrise. The Trogon (*Harpactes fasciatus*) has a black neck and head, blue bill, and yellow back; a bright red breast, and wings delicately pencilled with white lines on a black ground. Between this bird and the Kingfisher comes the Red-headed Barbet as a link, called by naturalists *Megalaima Indica*, but commonly known as the "coppersmith," from its call, exactly like the blows of a hammer upon a large metal pot. It is a dull heavy bird, with an unhappy look of sepulchral deliberation, and acts as if every movement were a worry to it. It has a peculiar habit of puffing out its feathers in a ball, whence it is sometimes called the "puff-bird."

The large yellow Woodpecker (*Brachypternus aurantius*) incessantly taps the dead trees in search of insects. At the top of lofty trees screams the Hornbill or Toucan (*Buceros malabaricus*), the flesh of which is eaten as a cure for rheumatism, and whose only drink is said to be falling rain.[1] Less obtrusive and better-behaved is the *Mi-kian* (*avitchia*), a red and green bird rather smaller than a crow, with a plaintive note resembling its name, and meaning "I *will* complain," a protest which it addresses to the rising sun in consequence of the theft of its tail-feathers by the peacock.

Among the Accipitres there is the Crested eagle (*Spizaetus limnaetus*), a great enemy of poultry among the hills; the Serpent eagle (*Hæmatornis bacha*), that feeds on reptiles in the marshes; and the Great Sea Erne (*Ponto-*

[1] Note O.

aetus leucogaster) or Brahminy Kite, often to be seen hunting on the beach at low tide in company with the sacred Fishing Eagle (*Haliastur Indicus*).

Next come the Hawks, among which are lovely but rare Peregrine Falcons (*F. peregrinus*), the Sparrow-hawk (*Accipiter badius*), almost as plentiful as in Europe, and the audacious Kestrel (*Tinnunculus alaudarius*) ; as well as the Goshawk (*Astur trivirgatus*), that swoops and wheels round precipitous crags. Near Anuradhapoora this bird is trained for hunting with its eyes darkened. Along the shore, enjoying a feast of dead fish, are to be seen many Kites (*Milvus govinda*), ignoble birds of prey.

The commonest Owl is the Indranee (*Syrnium indranee*), called by the Buddhists *ulama* or devil-bird, a handsome brown, 3 feet across the wings, twice as large as the British Barn-owl. It is said to be a metamorphosed woman, who was compelled by her husband to eat her babe; it has a strange cry, of which an Englishman who has heard it says, "I heard piercing and convulsive screams so horribly agonising that it was difficult to believe murder was not being committed."

There is a handsome specimen of the "devil-bird" in the Zoological Gardens in Regent's Park close to the north entrance, as there is also of the Fish-owl (*Ketupa Zeylonensis*), a tall thin bird with wonderful yellow eyes. A pretty little owl peculiar to Ceylon is *Athene castanotus*, called by the natives *puncha barra*, with a wing only 5 inches long.

Among the Passeres the Swallow (*Collocalia nidifica*) is the most important; it builds the edible nest of which considerable quantities are exported by the Chinese, who have a small settlement for that purpose on the west coast.

Where the river sweeps round a projecting rock the tiny red-billed Kingfisher (*ceÿx tridactyla*) sits sunning itself, with feathers rivalling the blue of the sapphire sky. No words can describe the splendour of this little beauty. The back is a deep rich lilac, the wing feathers are stained in the centre with deep blue, on the edge with ultramarine, while all underneath is pure white. To add to his glory he has red feet and a pale carmine bill.

Hovering round the garden flowers is to be seen the Sun-bird, or humming-bird of Ceylon

(*Nectarina zeylanica*) ; while from many a bough hangs the nest of the Weaver-bird (*Ploceus baya*), looking like a long-necked bottle, which, if we are to believe the natives, is lighted up at night by fireflies stuck round it inside. Even a more skilful workman is the sober little Tailor-bird (*Orthotomus longicaudus*), that makes a nest of marvellous ingenuity. Taking two leaves at the extremity of a slender twig the bird literally sews them together at their edge with home-made vegetable fibre thread, using its bill for a needle. Soft cottony down and a few feathers are then pushed in between the leaves, and a hollow is scraped out for the eggs and young. The nest is hung at the extremity of the thinnest twigs, in order to keep it safe from the prying attentions of monkeys and snakes.

To the same family belongs the Bulbul (*Pycnonotus hæmorrhous*), the tuft-bird or *kouda cooroola* of the natives, which in former days, on account of its extraordinary courage and obstinacy, used to be trained by the Kandyan kings for fighting purposes. It is not to be confounded with the bulbul of Persian poetry, which is probably nothing else than the true nightingale of Europe.

The proletariat Crow is found everywhere, a most impudent and voracious thief. It is a sight towards evening to see the crows enjoying a fresh-water bath in the tank by the Fort at Colombo. The commonest in towns is *Corvus splendens*, a glossy black bird shot with blue. In the country *C. culminatus* swarms, and is often to be seen with its curious convex bill perched upon the back of a buffalo side by side with the small tick-loving *minah*. Tennent mentions an instance in which a crow untied a knot in a paper parcel, while another extracted the peg which fastened the lid of a basket. An instance of their prying curiosity came under my own notice. When I was staying in the Queen's Hotel at Kandy, I was awoke one morning as usual very early by the *appo* or "boy" bringing in my *chota hazeri*, a little breakfast consisting of tea, toast, and jam. The night had been intensely hot, and doors and windows had been left wide open. On looking round I saw a droll-looking crow hopping about the room, evidently in search of curios for breakfast. I watched him lazily until he hopped solemnly on to the dressing-table and began to peck inquisitively at a few trinkets lying there. Knowing the thievish propensities of his race I thought it time to interfere, and jumped out of bed to drive him away. This, however, I found to be a difficult feat. First under the chairs, then under the couch and the bed, he dodged my pursuit, always perching just where he knew I could not reach him. Nor did he think proper to retire from the contest until he had obtained possession of a broad elastic band which had encircled my diary, and with which he hopped triumphantly out of the room and down the stairs, evidently under the delusion that he had captured a choice specimen of a newly-imported earthworm. I never ascertained the fate of that bird, but there can be little room for conjecture, if he went so far as to make his morning meal off what must have proved, even to an Indian crow, a tough and gruesome morsel. It is a Singhalese saying that the soul of a rice-stealer passes into the body of a crow, a theory for which I think there is much to be said.[1]

The Scansores are represented in Ceylon chiefly by the Psittacidæ, of which one species, the Parroquet (*Palæornis Alexandri*), is in vast numbers. Doves and pigeons are also common.

[1] Note P.

One of the Columbidæ (*Chalcophaps Indicus*), called by the Singhalese *neela-cobeya*, has a charming low melodious voice with a strangely soothing effect, to which many travellers have borne witness.

A species of Jungle Fowl (*Gallus Lafayetti*) is the only member of the Gallinæ, and is peculiar to Ceylon, where it is very common and quite different from the Indian varieties. No specimen has ever been brought alive to Europe. It has a singular cry, heard at sunrise, which sounds like the words *George Joyce.*

In far greater numbers than any of these are the Grallæ, of which multitudes frequent the lagoons and marshes, waders, ibises (*Tantalus leucocephalus*), storks (*Ciconia leucocephala*), spoonbills (*Platalea leucorodia*), herons (*Ardea purpurea*), plovers, and sand-larks, which swarm on the wet sea-sand searching for the red worm.

To these I must add the Anseres, tall long-legged Flamingoes (*Phœnicopterus roseus*), often called "English soldiers," which stand with their white backs and crimson underwings (only seen when they rise) in long files along the margin of the waves. There are also teal innumerable (*Nettapus Coromandelicus*), gulls (*Larus brunni-*

cephalus), ducks and shovellers (*Spatula clypeata*), terns (*Sterna minuta*), and flocks of pelicans (*P. Philippensis*).

In my rambles I often came across birds more familiar than most of these, such as partridges, quail, woodcock, pheasant (a spurious variety), and snipe. These last give splendid shooting from October to April (being migratory from India), and are very pretty birds, with smooth round little heads, beady eyes, and graceful markings, perfect little aristocrats, and not quite so quick on the wing as in England. The "painted snipe" is very common, with a large dark eye, just like a woodcock's, a fine chocolate-coloured head, broad white collar, back and wings shaded green, and the pen-feathers marked with gold spots.

Exaggerated descriptions of the Reptilia of Ceylon have from time to time found their way into print from the reports of imaginative and too credulous travellers. But when all allowance has been made for what are specifically known as "snake stories," the fact remains that the presence of the ophidians forms a distinct drawback to the pleasure of living in many parts of the island. I have a personal acquaintance with Australian and Tasmanian snakes, neither of which can, I think, compare with those of Ceylon either for number or venom.

The number of different varieties of snakes is given as between forty and fifty, of which eight live more or less in trees, two in fresh water, and eight in salt. All are carnivorous, but fortunately not equally dangerous. The sea-snakes are all deadly, as are those on land whose fangs are perforated. These are: 1. Cobra (*Naja tripudians*). 2. Tic polonga (*Daboia Russellii*), called by the natives *katuka*. 3. Carawilla (*Trigonocephalus hypnalis*), known commonly as *mala*. 4. Green Carawilla (*Trimeresurus trigonocephalus*). All the rest are harmless, at least to man.

The Cobra, hooded or spectacled snake, of which there are fifteen varieties, is from 4 to 6 feet long and of thick girth, with dark spots on a pale ground. On its head are marks round the eyes resembling a pair of spectacles, all the more singular when we know that although gifted with very acute hearing, its sight is very dull. The fangs are weak, so much so that they are unable to penetrate clothing, for which reason natives suffer far more than Europeans, who have never been known to die from its bite. This snake has received a great deal of attention at the hands of naturalists, in consequence of a curious belief, which it is difficult to relegate entirely to the region of imagination, to the effect that a certain number of the species carry about with them a small shining stone in their mouths. The following description is taken in substance from a curious paper on the *Naja-kalu*, or cobra stone, by Professor Hensoldt, in *Harper's New Monthly Magazine* for March 1890, to which I would refer all who desire more information. I may say at the outset that the stone is said to be the size of a pea, round, and semi-opaque, and with a power of shining in the dark. The natives affirm that at night the cobra puts the stone upon the ground, and watches it as if fascinated, being ready to defend it with its life against all comers.

Professor Hensoldt when in Ceylon determined to find out the truth, an old planter having told him that he had seen as many as forty cobras in possession of the stone. By the offer of a reward, the Professor was led by a Tamul coolie one night to the edge of a stream, where under a huge tamarind tree a cobra was lying, swaying its head slowly to and fro, close to a tiny greenish light, which did not fade at regular intervals, as does the light of the fire-fly (*Lampyris noctiluca*), but shone with an uninterrupted steady glow. As there was nothing at hand with which to kill the snake, the coolie promised to procure it the next night by a plan which he said could not fail. He kept his word, and in due time brought the *naja-kalu*, a water-worn yellow pebble, oval and flattened, and emitting a green phosphorescent light. The Professor found it to be a rare variety of fluor spar, known as chlophane, a mineral so sensitive that it will shine when merely warmed by the hand. The Tamul told him he had climbed the tree and taken up a position exactly over the spot where the snake had lain the night before. Directly the cobra appeared and had deposited the stone on the grass, the coolie emptied a bag of ashes over it, by which means the reptile was prevented from regaining the treasure. After a while it departed, and the man secured his prize. The explanation of this apparent marvel may be that the cobra has a special liking for fire-flies, the females of which alone shine, while the males fly round them, and from time to time settle close to them. There seems to be little doubt that the *naja-kalu* is used by the cobra as a decoy. All it has to do is to deposit the stone, and the attracted fire-flies come within easy reach. Perhaps also, as its own sight is feeble, the shining stone may serve as a sort of range-finder.

Another and less rational belief among the natives is that all snakes belong to another world, and are akin to the gods; for which reason they refrain from killing them, although they do not scruple to put them in bags and fling them into any water that is handy.

The Tic (or spotted) Polonga is a rock snake living chiefly in deserted nests of the white ant, but frequently found climbing trees in search of birds' nests. It is from 4 to 6 feet long, with thick body, gray back, and yellow belly. It is of indolent habits, but venomous enough to kill a fowl in sixty seconds, or a dog in the same number of minutes.

The Carawilla is a dusky red snake with white belly, from 1 to 2 feet in length. A friend told me that on taking hold of what he thought was a stick lying upon his pianoforte, he found it was a carawilla, whose back he promptly broke by cracking it like a whip. A lady told me that as she was stepping one evening into her carriage, a snake of the same species glided leisurely off the cushion. A green carawilla which I killed near Nuwara Eliya was 2 feet 3 inches long.

Of all Ceylon snakes the largest is the harmless and common Indian Rock snake, known as the Python (*P. molurus*), or Ceylon boa. The Hindoos call it *pedda-poda.* It is black and yellow, and from 12 to 18 feet long. Rat-snakes (*Pytas muscosus*) are of medium size, very common and harmless, fond of preying upon rats and other vermin, for which purpose they glide about the roofs, and now and then find their way into the rooms through the ceiling.

There are large numbers of Tree or Whip snakes, averaging 3 feet, with pointed nose, large eyes, and body no thicker than the lash of a whip. They move like lightning and are of different hues—green, yellow, bronze, or purple. I shot a rare and handsome one (*Passerita fusca*), the colour of which was shining brown shot with purple. *P. mycterizans* is a very beautiful dark blue and brown wood snake, about 3 feet in length, living in trees upon birds, and furnished with a curious appendage to its snout, covered with scales, the use of which is unknown.

The Sea-snake (*Hydrophis*) is always deadly, and is found in great numbers all round the coast, especially in the Gulf of Manaar, from 1 to 3 feet long, of a greenish hue tending to yellow, some specimens being also banded with black.[1]

It has been reserved for Dr. Müller of Victoria to settle the exact merits of strychnine as an antidote to snake poison. The proper application is one part of nitrate of strychnine dissolved in 240 parts of water mixed with a little glycerine, which must be injected under the skin as near the bitten part as possible. In the many cases which he has successfully treated Dr. Müller has had no hesitation in using the drug when necessary in quantities that would have been fatal in the absence of the antagonistic venom.

A rare and little-known creature, classed by some as one of the Pseudophidia or false snakes, but more probably a batrachian, is the Cæcilia (*C. glutinosa*), found in rocky jungle ground near

[1] Note Q.

Kandy. It has a long cylindrical body without limbs, 2 feet long and 1 inch thick, with a flat head and almost invisible eye (whence its name signifying blindness). It is covered with minute scales, and emits a viscous fluid from its pores like a snail.

To these I may add a worm (*Megascolex cæruleus*), a curiosity of the Ceylon fauna found in the north. It measures no less than 60 inches in length and 1 in thickness, and is of a light blue colour. I have seen even this giant surpassed in Australia by one at least a foot longer (*M. Australensis*).

Crocodiles grow to an immense size, and are very numerous and prolific in certain districts. They are commonly spoken of as alligators (derived from the Portuguese *lagarto*), of which there is no example in Ceylon. The alligator has a broader head and shorter snout than the crocodile, as well as numerous other scientific variations, especially in the teeth and legs. Crocodiles literally swarm in the low marshy lands, and are of two kinds—*C. biporcatus* or common crocodile (in Singhalese *eli-kimboola*), and *C. palustris*. The former is the larger and fiercer, often measuring 16 or 18 feet in length; the smaller marsh crocodile is sly and cowardly, and rarely exceeds 12 feet. The largest crocodiles are found at Batticaloa. The common idea that the reptile is very susceptible to titillation is perfectly correct; it has been known to relax its hold on a man who, when fast in its jaws, managed to rub its under side gently with his hand. During a long drought the crocodile usually buries itself in the mud, where it remains in a state of torpor until the rain comes. The teeth of the larger kind are used by the natives, mounted with silver, as chunam boxes.

Nowhere are larger Saurians to be found than in Ceylon. The largest is an iguana (*Hydrosaurus*), the native *kabara*, or *kabra*, *goya*, found in the marshes from 8 to 10 feet long. It is immensely tenacious of life, and is armed with a strong sharp-ridged tail plated with mail. The Singhalese, who eat most things from an ant to an elephant, pronounce it uneatable, although they eat the smaller iguanas, which, as I can testify, are much like veal in flavour. They use the fat as a remedy in skin maladies, and from other parts prepare a deadly poison called *kabara-tel*, often called *cobra-tel* by Europeans, who wrongly confound it with snake-poison. The deadly effects of this preparation, which are undoubted, seem to be due chiefly to the large quantity of arsenic which is added.

Some of my readers may remember old Peter Martyr's description of the disgust of the brother of Columbus, Don Bartolomeo Colon, and his suite at Xaragua, when the American "Indians" first set before them the iguana as a banquet dish: "Their serpentes," he says, "are lyke unto crocodiles, save in bygness; they call them guanas. Unto that day none of owre men durste adventure to taste of them, by reason of theyre horrible deformitie and lothsomness. Yet the Adelantado being entysed by the pleasantnes of the king's sister Anacaona, determined to taste the serpentes. But when he felte the flesh thereof to be so delycate to his tongue, he fel to amayne without al feare. The which thyng his companions perceiving were not behynde hym in greedynesse: insomuche that they had now none other talk than of the sweetnesse of these serpentes, which they affirm be of more pleasant taste than eyther our phesantes or partriches."

Another variety of iguana is *Monitor dracæna* or *talla-goya*, small, and sometimes hunted by dogs, and turned into a curry by no means to be despised. I have often watched a *talla-goya* busy at work up and down a hedge-ridge after insects. The natives take out the tongue from the living animal and use it as a cure for consumption.

The Chameleon (*C. vulgaris*) is found, but not as commonly as some suppose, in the middle and northern parts of the island. It is of a blue-ash colour, which it can change at will to a green or yellow hue with red spots. The eyes are projecting, and can be turned in any direction quite independently of each other. It moves along the branches of trees in a lazy fashion, but when it gets a victim within range darts out its broad cuneiform tongue, which is literally longer than its body, with inconceivable swiftness.

With the same power of changing colour is found *Calotes versicolor*, a lovely reptile of brilliant emerald green, a foot long, with jaws of such power that it is impossible to detach them from a stick. From the red hue which it sometimes assumes it has received the misleading name of "blood-snake."

The only other lizards I have myself seen in Ceylon were some very pretty ones at Peredeniya, of a greenish-brown, with pale blue bellies, known as "lyre-heads."

The Gecko (*Hemidactylus maculatus* and *H. frenatus*) is a strange piece of nature's handiwork of the lizard kind, very common in Colombo and the neighbourhood. It has large wild-looking eyes and very sharp claws, from which exudes a viscous fluid by means of which it scampers along a flat ceiling. It is quite harmless, a common bedroom companion, and a useful devourer of insects. I have often watched one standing patiently upon a wall, solemnly nodding its head until it saw a likely prey, upon which it would dart like lightning.

To the Cheloniadæ belong the Turtles, which are numerous, and whose eggs are sold for a few shillings, or sometimes pence. The edible turtle (*Chelonia virgata*) is found on the north coasts from 4 to 5 feet long, and is often to be seen exposed in the markets for sale, the flesh being cut from the live animal in morsels. I once saw a crowd gathered by the seaside round a turtle which was found to weigh 680 pounds, upon which I fed afterwards to the extent of about one ounce. The flesh is rather like poor beef. I found thirty or forty eggs one day in a nest under a tree just above high-water mark. The nest was nothing but a hollow in the sand deep enough to cover the creature entirely. In the middle was a hole bored straight down to the depth of 18 inches, and in which were the eggs. Usually they are difficult to find, but I surprised the "mother-bird" as she was coming up out of the water. When she saw me she turned and fled at an astonishing pace in a curious series of jerks from side to side, making short strokes with her flippers. A friend who was with me was speedy enough to catch her just as she was at the edge of the sea, and cut off her retreat. She was not a large one, but still weighed 218½ pounds. The eggs of the turtle are quite round, the size of a small billiard ball, with no shell but a kind of parchment covering. I have eaten many things between the Arctic circle and Van Diemen's Land, but never have I tasted anything half so nasty as a raw turtle's egg. The young turtles are hatched as big as a crown-piece, quite formed and ready for the devouring troubles of life, which soon come to many of them in the form of birds and crabs. The "bull" or male turtle is never found ashore, but is caught floating on the water.

Tortoise-shell is the carapace of *Caretta imbricata* or hawksbill, and is generally taken from the living animal in order to improve the colour: the poor creature is hung over a slow wood-fire until the shell falls off. The Moormen work the shell into many articles of use and beauty. Some of the land tortoises are of a handsome starred variety (*T. stellata*), generally found swarming upon the soft parts of the head and neck with ticks. The marshes and fresh-water pools are the home of Terrapins (*Cryptopus granum*), supposed to be endowed with the property of cleansing water from impurities. They live for a long time in captivity in a proper temperature if fed upon meat and water.

Among Batrachians there are enormous numbers of Frogs, including seven true species of webbed ones, five of tree ones (*polypedates*), and others. The commonest of all is *Hyla leucomystax*, a tree frog with the power of changing colour. It has a bell-like croak, and, like all its kind, has a round disk on the end of its toes by which it climbs. *Rana malabarica* is 8 inches long, olive green and brown on back, common in the Colombo lagoons. At Kandy I saw a much smaller frog (*R. Kandiana*) of a beautiful grass green with orange belly.

Toads are of two or three varieties, of which the handsomest is the Indian toad (*Bufo melanostictus*), common near the coast. The body is orange yellow spotted with black, and with a black head: when suddenly alarmed it turns red.

It will be evident that the waters in and around Ceylon are as full of life as the land, when we know that 600 different kinds of Fish have been catalogued. The Singhalese are fine expert fishermen, and catch plenty of sole, whiting, mackerel, carp, red mullet, perch, seir, and sardines, as well as a host of red, blue, yellow, and lustrous green fish known as "parrots" or *giraway*. It is impossible by words to give any idea of the absolute splendour of some of these latter.[1] Among the especially gorgeous ones are the Flower-parrot or *mal-girawali* (*Sparus Hard-*

[1] The reader will find many of them excellently set forth in colours in J. W. Bennett's *Fishes of Ceylon* (London, 1830).

wickii), marked with irregular horizontal bands of blue, crimson, purple, yellow, and gray, crossed by six dark perpendicular ones from top of back to belly; on the head are broad red and green radii from the eye. The Great Fire-fish (*Scorpæna volitans* or *Pterois muricata*), the native *gini-maha*, is of a bright flame-colour, 4 or 5 inches long and with a white nutritious flesh. The Linnæan name of this fish is a misleading one, inasmuch as the pectoral fins do not admit of flight. The *Seweya* (*Acanthurus vittatus*), 16 inches long, is a most brilliant fish, with blue and yellow stripes drawn from head to tail, and a sharp curved spine which it can erect at pleasure. The *ratoo*, or red, *pahaya* is a bright red fish, 2 feet long, plentiful off Galle and excellent eating; when just taken from the water nothing can exceed the splendour of its colour. The *kaha-bartikyah* is a tiny creature with yellow body and fins. Of a beautiful smalt hue is another pigmy *Chætodon Brownriggii*. The *deweeborawoowah* is a most handsome fellow, 18 inches long, brilliant yellow with strong brown horizontal lines; and the *hembili girawah* or Basket parrot (*S. decussatus*) is a foot long, marked with singular gay squares just like basket plait-work, from which it gets its native name.

Best of all for edible use is the Seir (*Cybium guttatum*), or *tora-malu*, a large flat fish of the Scomberidæ family, with white flesh and a flavour like salmon.[1] Oysters are poor, shapeless, and knotty, hardly better eating than the sharks, from which an oil is extracted, and whose fins make a soup no less dear to the palate of a Chinaman than is the *bêche-de-mer* or sea-slug, of which large quantities, in size from 2 to 12 inches, are exported from Trincomalee.[2] Sardines are said to be at certain seasons poisonous. In 1824 the Government evidently thought so, for Sir E. Barnes made an order forbidding their use by the troops during the months of December and January.

Two or three varieties of Saw-fish (*Pristis antiquorum*) are found, a fish that is common from the Arctic Circle to the Line, measuring in the Indian Ocean from 12 to 18 feet, and armed with a sharp serrated beak or rostrum, with which it mangles the pearl-diver, or runs amuck through a shoal of smaller fry. Huge as these

[1] Note R. [2] Note S.

are, they are surpassed sometimes by the Sword-fish (*Histiophorus immaculatus*), 20 feet long, whose dark violet-coloured dorsal fin is un-spotted, and both higher than and different in hue from the blue-spotted one in the Atlantic and Mediterranean fish.

The Cheironectes belongs to the queer and clever family of Lophiades or "anglers," of which specimens are not unknown in European waters. It not only walks along the sea-sand like a quadruped, but sports a small worm-like excrescence upon the top of its head, which it waggles about in the water to attract the foolish little fishes to their destruction. The Red Perch (*Holocentum rubrum*) is a gaudy fish, and closes my list of salt-water ones.

As to the number of the fish living in fresh water old Robert Knox bears witness: "Every ditch," he says, "and little plash of water but ankle-deep hath fish in it." Carp, barbel, perch, gray mullet, etc., are seldom eaten, but an exception must be made in favour of the eels (Singhalese *theliya*), many of which, both in sea and fresh water, are excellent.

There is one fish which may correctly be called

an amphibious one, the Climbing Perch (*Anabas scandens*), 6 inches long, and supplied with certain pharyngeal bones which retain a store of moisture. Thus by exuding moisture the gills are kept damp while the fish takes a walk on shore. It leaves the pools and nullahs in the dry season, and makes its way overland to the nearest water. Closely allied to this are the burying fish, and the fish that falls from the clouds, and singing fish, and many other marvels of which I have no personal knowledge.[1] No less interesting are two species *Apogon* and *Ambassis*, which find life worth living in the hot springs of Kannea near Trincomalee, the temperature of which is often 122°: well may they rejoice in their specific name of *thermalis*. They are surpassed, however, by fish living in a hot spring of 187° Fahrenheit at Manilla, and by those seen by Humboldt in South America thrown up alive by a volcano at a temperature of 210°, just 2° short of boiling point.

I am not acquainted with the proper scientific name for a horde of ridiculous little fishes which actually attacked me one morning when I was

[1] Note T.

enjoying a dip in a mountain stream, hundreds of them, mere minnows, doing their best to nibble the flesh off my bones.

On the margin of that beautiful ocean, whose league-long billows break at the feet of the palms, are to be found many Crustaceans, which I may be excused for speaking of here out of their proper order. On the south side of Colombo harbour, and I daresay in a thousand other spots within the tropic of Cancer, are lovely little Painted Crabs (*Grapsus strigosus*), which scutter swiftly about in their yellow shells dappled with red. Calling-crabs also scamper over the sand, each one looking as if it were beckoning you with an uplifted hand larger than its whole body. One kind, resembling the climbing *agavule* of Fiji, live on land near the sea, making burrows in the earth and feeding upon coco-nuts. They break through the eye of the nut with their pincers, and are handy at grabbing any human extremity that gets in their way. It is well to remember that if you are nipped, you can free yourself by tickling the crab, as if it were an alligator, upon the under side of its anatomy. Black Sea-urchins are quite ready to thrust into your foot a spine 12 inches long, with prickles all set the wrong way, the said spine having a nasty habit of breaking short off and leaving a painful wound. Paddle-crabs (*Remipes testudinarius*), Pea-crabs (*Pinnotheres pisum*), and the vagabond Hermit (*Cenobita Diogenes*) are all close at hand, as well as the Prawn and Shrimp.

From crawling shrimp to light and airy butterfly seems a long jump. But as Articulata, our old friends, so suggestive of Greenwich and watercress, are closely allied with the gaudy Lepidoptera. A good many people, otherwise well informed, know nothing about butterflies; not a few would be at a loss to say offhand what are the distinguishing characteristics of butterflies and moths. It was but the other day that at a German custom-house an entomologist's collection of butterflies was detained, on the ground that because they had wings they were poultry, and must therefore pay duty as such.

Even in these over-educated days there may be here and there a very young child who is not aware of the similarity existing between the structure of a butterfly and that of a crustacean.

In both the heart is situated in the back, the digestive organs are in the middle, the nervous system is underneath; whereas in man, birds, fishes, reptiles, and all mammals, the nervous system is placed in the back, the digestive organs are in the middle, and the heart is in front. Moreover, the body of a shrimp is built in compartments exactly resembling those in the interior of a butterfly.

Butterflies are less numerous in Ceylon than one would expect to find. But among them are some of the most splendid in the world. Where is there a more superb insect than the black and yellow *Ornithoptera darsius*, 6 inches across the wings? or the Hector (*Papilio H.*), glorious in black velvet swallow-tailed wings with crimson spots, and measuring 4 inches; or the blue and black *Amathusa philarchus*? Another black and blue one, *P. polymnestor*, pays constant court to the yellow hibiscus. In one stage of its existence this insect is decidedly obnoxious. The Dutch during their occupation cut several canals, along the banks of which they planted the *Hibiscus populneus*. To these trees with their broad leaves the streets of Colombo owe much of their coolness and shade. But unfortunately they are the home of the hairy green-striped caterpillar of *P. polymnestor*, which is apt to descend by a silky thread upon the unwary passers-by, in whose bare skin it inflicts a wound far worse than a nettle or star-fish.

The Sylph (*Hestia Jasonia*), or Spectre, may often be seen flying gracefully over a pool in the shady forest, whither at the setting of the sun come also swarms of *Hesperidæ*, attracted by the sweet champac or moon-flower. When night has settled down, the moths begin to flutter about, and the petals of the periwinkle are stirred by the hum of the Hawk-moth. There are no lovelier insects in the world than the superb white Moon-moth of the Bombycidæ tribe; or the brown Atlas (*Phalæna A.*), often 10 inches across, that haunts the Cinnamon Gardens in Colombo; or the Death's-head moth (*Acherontia satanas*), with a perfect "death's head" upon its shoulders, in colour a rich brown marked like tortoise-shell. Inferior in size but not in beauty is the Tusseh Silk-moth (*Antheræa mylitta*), whose favourite food is the castor-oil plant.

Coleoptera are strongly represented. Beetles

are many and are frequently eaten by the natives, the greatest delicacy being the larvæ of the Coco-nut beetle, called by them *gascooroominiya*. This taste they share with the ancient Israelites, to whom Moses gave express permission to eat beetles (Levit. xi. 22). The Coco-nut beetle (*Oryctes rhinoceros*) perforates the young palm and forms a cocoon of wood and sawdust. Although to a native a beetle is a delicacy as food, it is more than he can endure to see a live one in his house after nightfall. Believing it to be sent by some enemy known or unknown for his destruction, he expels it with the greatest care, in the hope that if not injured it will find its way back to the sender laden with retaliation.

The Scavenger-beetle (*Ateuchus sacer*) has a curious habit of fastening upon putrescent matter, cutting it up into lumps, and burying it with its own eggs inside.

There is no more wonderful instance of the imitative power of nature than one of the Orthoptera, known as *Phyllium siccofolium*, or Walking-leaf-insect. There are many varieties of the Mantis or Leaf-insect in Ceylon, but none more astonishing than this. It is the most perfect imitation of a pale yellow, green, or brown leaf, the wings modelled like ribbed and fibrous follicles; each joint of the legs expanded into a broad plait like a half-open leaf, and its eggs not to be distinguished from seeds. Lying perfectly flat along the surface of a leaf, it defies detection. Other kinds are the Stick insect, a veritable spectre; and the Soothsayer or Praying Mantis (*M. superstitiosa*), with a certain appearance of gentle sanctity, which, however, is delusive, seeing that it is an inveterate cannibal. In this instance, as in so many others, we see that the insects of Ceylon, like the flora, have a closer affinity with those of Australia than with those of India.

Cockroaches, grasshoppers, and cicadas, which from their strident music have earned the name of "knife-grinders," are all in tens of thousands; and scarcely less in number are the graceful dragonflies, which flash over the surface of stream and pool, revelling, unlike most other insects, in the fiercest heat of noon. One variety (*Euphæa splendens*) is of a brilliant emerald hue. The larvæ may be seen in the tanks, propelling themselves along by sucking in water at one end and driving it out at the other. To this same family belongs also the Ant-lion (*Myrmeleon gravis*), of which there are four species peculiar to the island. This insect digs a conical pit an inch deep, and hides at the bottom: result, death to ants. Here too must be included an insect whose room is much to be preferred to its company in all tropical lands, the White Ant, which is no true ant at all but a termite (*T. Taprobanes*), half an inch long and milky white. Its destructive ravages are well known. Buildings have been erected of the most massive timber, and been deserted because of the impossibility of expelling it. When at work it covers its operations with a tubing of clay, until without any outward sign of decay the whole mass becomes mere sawdust. The only Ceylon woods that will resist white ants are ebony, ironwood, and palmyra palm. Their home is a conical structure of impervious clay, in shape like a sugarloaf from 3 to 6 feet high: indeed they sometimes rise to double that height. Inside it is full of cells and compartments with connecting galleries, like the nests of bees, which the white ant in its notions of home-rule much resembles. It is no wonder that it is found a difficult matter to get rid of them, when we know that the queen termite lays 3,000,000 eggs every year. At certain times these pests swarm like gnats in the air, being furnished with wings which after a while drop off. It is difficult sometimes in the tropics to read or write after the lamp is lit at night, the white ants swarming over everything, in numbers rivalling the mosquito.

Among Hymenoptera the Mason-flies, of bright metallic lustre, are found of all sizes from a gnat to a hornet, and of such singular courage that a tiny one will assault and vanquish a cockroach. Their nests are marvels of sagacious industry, the interior consisting of oval cells of clay, in which the eggs are laid, and a store of captured spiders preserved as food for their young. Their commissariat department sometimes overflows into queer places such as gun-barrels and keys. This insect has an objectionable habit also of filling up keyholes with clay, where it deposits the pupa of another insect, inside whose carcase it has already secreted its own eggs. One of the same family (*Sphex ferruginea*) builds a nest hanging 6 feet in length from a branch, and is much dreaded by the natives for its terrible sting.

Most of the Ceylon Bees are stingless. There are five kinds in all, of which four are honey-makers, the wax being bartered by the aboriginal Veddahs for clothing, arrow-heads, etc. The Carpenter bee (*Xylocopa tenuiscapa*), bright green, with sheeny purple wings, and as big as a walnut, possesses a sting, unlike his fellows, but makes no honey. The Bambera is a large honey bee, whose pendent nest looks just like a Cheshire cheese; its wax is very pure and white, and fully equal to the famed *miel vert* of the Ile de Bourbon.

Luminous insects in Ceylon are found in several species, of which the brightest is a fat, comfortable-looking, white grub, 2 inches long, by whose light the smallest print may be read. The Eye-flies, on the other hand, possess a real blinding power, often flying in scores into the eyes, and putting a stop to the labours of the artist or botanist.

In Ceylon, which by virtue of its possession of 10,000 varieties may be called the headquarters of the insect world, the entomologist may in the course of a short stroll become the possessor of a fine miscellaneous collection of insects upon his own person, including ticks, mosquitoes, leeches, spiders, and ants. Of these last there are incredible numbers, which swarm everywhere, from the oil of a bedroom lamp to the topmost branches of the tallest tree. There is a black ant (*Formica nigra*), a busy and useful scavenger, that makes a clean sweep of all dead beetles, cockroaches, lizards, etc. The largest kind, with jaws that give a really formidable bite, is called by the Singhalese *kalu-koombiya*. Most of the black ones live upon the ground, unlike the red ones, which build their nests in trees. There is a large red ant (*F. smaragdina*) very abundant in gardens and fruit trees, called by the natives *dimiya*, a fierce and combative insect, with serrated mandibles. Another smaller one (*F. nidificans*) makes a tree-nest which looks just like a paper-bag. Some of these ants are really a power to be reckoned with. To a coolie picking mangoes, with nothing but a bit of woollen stuff round his loins, half a dozen soldier ants are no joke. In the jungle they often fall upon the wayfarer with absolute fury, inflicting an intensely painful bite. They are not a bit less vicious than the Australian "bull-dog" ants, which go recklessly for your boot or walking-stick, and are, in proportion to their size, without doubt the most pugnacious and audacious of all living things.

Fleas and Bugs, the former particularly, surpass the sands of the sea for multitude. Ticks (*Oribata* and *Ixodes*) swarm in countless hordes in the low brushwood of the plains, and fastening upon their victim promptly insert a barbed proboscis, burrowing with their heads under the skin and producing an intolerable smarting. I have often torn off the body, but the head has remained in the wound and made a nasty sore. The best remedy I found to be a drop of coco-oil or lime-juice. They are a perfect torment also to dogs and cattle, as they are cunning enough to settle upon the eyebrows, ear-tips, or back of the neck, just where they are least easily got rid of.

I write the word Diptera with an involuntary shudder, for does it not include that bane of all hot countries, the Mosquito (*Culex laniger*)? No pen can describe its fearsomeness, the same all the world over, only worse just in the particular place one happens to be in. High up within the Arctic Circle in the merry month of June I have ministered to its deathless thirst; under the Line in sultry December have I battled with its singing legions; in Queensland all the year round I have cursed it; in Ajaccio not once nor twice I have bespattered the white wall of my little *casa* with blood drawn from my own veins. It will be understood therefore that I consider myself a competent authority upon the subject of mosquitoes; and it has often formed a matter of wondering conjecture in my mind, how small must be the number of these "wailful gnats," which are ever tempted by human blood, compared with those myriads which in their native swamps know not the taste of it. And when they do come into contact with men, their cunning and strategy are such that it seems to be beyond a doubt that the proper study of mosquitoes is man. They are daring and bloodthirsty creatures, a noisy and nipping crew, who will take no denial. Neither the strength of Samson nor the patience of Job can avail anything against these "thorns in the flesh." A mosquito-net, at least in Ceylon, is next to useless, owing not less to its usually tattered condition than to the superhuman sagacity of the foe. It is all very well to imagine that mosquitoes can be dodged with vermin powder. My firm belief is, after much study of their ways, that they thrive and do well upon it. It is a futile expenditure of time and trouble to kill *a* mosquito; they are as reckless of life as Zulus, nor would any amount of slaughter sensibly diminish their hordes. It is commonly said of them in Ceylon, as of the fleas in Egypt, that they are strong enough when caught to kick your hand open. For my own part, I prefer the large ones to the small.

The world is waiting more or less patiently for the solution of two problems—the abolition of sea-sickness and the extermination of mosquitoes. We have our remedies and our preventives for each evil, but what are they worth? If we tuck in our net with the utmost care all round and jump into bed like a harlequin through a small gap, do we imagine that we are going to have the bed to ourselves? It might be so did not enough mosquitoes dart in also to make sleep an impossible thing. Their jubilant song soon sounds, and the weary hours of the hot night are spent in slapping instead of sleeping. The only variation comes from an occasional savage scratch, where a mosquito has raised a mound to her memory. Truth compels me to use the feminine gender, since it is an ascertained fact in natural history that the male insect is innocuous. Long before daybreak in Ceylon I used to rise impressed with the truth that it would require a great deal of investigation to work a mosquito into its proper place in the economy of nature.

Singhalese Spiders are only less numerous than ants, and in some instances attain proportions imposing enough to alarm the soul of the most valorous Miss Muffit. I ceased to be astonished at their numbers after finding near Damboola a small white ball, no larger than a pea, which turned out to be a silky bag, enwrapping as I supposed the ova of a spider, and made of closely interwoven threads with a glazed exterior. Inside, however, were no eggs, but a colony of young spiders fully formed, which I took out one by one to the number of 241.

The biggest Arachnid I ever saw was one called a *democulo* (*Mygale fasciata*), brown and hairy, with blotches and bands, 8 inches across the legs, a most noisome-looking creature. Without net or web *M. avicularia* is commonly said to compass the capture and drink the blood of small birds, as does the *Epeira diadema* of Australia. Another, *Olios Taprobanius*, covers an area of 3 inches, and is gray, with fiery red underneath; it spins a web like yellow silk, 2½ feet across, strong enough to catch and hold a walking-stick. Two species peculiar to Ceylon are a yellow four-eyed spider (*Miagrammopes*) and a blind yellow-brown one (*Tartarides*) found among dead leaves.

Of Myriapoda there are multitudes round Colombo and in all the low country, red or brown in colour, and covered with horny plates. The Tarantula as found in the island is small and harmless. It is as rapid a traveller as the milleped Cermatia, a most curious harmless insect with multitudinous feet, upon which it darts up and down the walls in search of flies and spiders; it is 12 inches long and marked with rich brown rings. Some of this tribe, however, are to be approached with caution, as I came upon some near Anuradhapoora which burnt to the touch like a stinging nettle, and looked just like a coiled spring of fine wire. Centipedes (*Scolopendræ*) are combative and obnoxious. *S. crassa* is nearly a foot long, with a dark purple body covered with armour and yellow legs. *S. pallipes* is a small dull green one. The Depisma, or Silver-fish, bears an evil reputation on account of its ravages among clothes, books, papers, etc. It is but fair to say that by some this pretty insidious little creature is supposed to be in itself harmless, or even beneficial as the destroyer of the larvæ of moths and other insects.

The Scorpion family are numerous and frequently annoying. I have caught black ones 5 inches long, the sting of which is more painful than dangerous, producing numbness, fever, and dizziness. *Buthus afer* advances towards you with an impudent air, cocking its articulated tail, in which is a crooked sting, with openings through which venom is squirted. A harmless species, *Scorpio linearis* or *Zeylanicus*, is yellow, narrow, and flat, 2 inches in length. Scorpions of all kinds (possibly because their deeds are evil) have a great horror of light, and are fond of avoiding observation in a glove or boot or under the bed-pillow. It is said, but with what truth I know not, that if they are surrounded by a ring of fire they will sting themselves to death.

I will close this chapter with the mention of a far more obnoxious individual, one of the Annelidæ, commonly known as the Leech (*Hæmadipsa Zeylanica*), than which there is no more detested pest in the island. In a recent book of travels I have seen its performances rather discounted, but I can only suppose that the writer's experiences must have been far more favourable than my own. Its favourite haunts are jungles and all low-lying damp land. It is an inch or so long, and when empty as thin as a thread, but quickly swells to the size of a quill when surfeited with blood. It can and does find its way through the finest stocking, and falls noiselessly upon the wayfarer from the boughs of trees. In many of the chenars it is impossible to walk in peace without strong cloth leech-gaiters drawn over the feet. It is a good plan to paint a ring of carbolic acid round the leg just above the boot. On the ground leeches rear themselves up on one end to watch for their victim. I have seen them hanging on the ankles of a coolie like a bunch of red cherries. The bite is a source of less danger than inconvenience, unless the victim happen to be in a state of bad health. One kind (*Hæmopsis paludum*) bothers the cattle on the alluvial lands, lurking among the rank vegetation or under a broad leaf, and fastening upon the nostrils, whence it sometimes penetrates to the mucous membranes of the throat. A dozen have been found in a bullock's gullet, of course causing death. This kind cannot pierce human skin, although it has been known to make a painful wound in the nostrils of a man while drinking.

Friar Odoricus, a Minorite, who visited Ceylon in the fourteenth century, speaks in his journal of the annoyance caused by these troublesome insects: "This water," he says, "is ful of hors-leeches and bloodsuckers, and of precious stones also, which the king taketh not unto his owne use, but once or twice every yere he permitteth certaine poore people to dive under the water for the said stones, and al that they can get he bestoweth upon them, to the end they may pray for his soule. But that they may with lesse danger dive under the water, they take limons which they pil, anointing themselves throughly with the juice thereof, and so they may dive naked under the water, the hors-leeches not being able to hurt them."[1]

I will conclude this imperfect sketch of animal life in Ceylon by a mention of the myriad Infusoria, which during the prevalence of a south-west monsoon often give a bright red tint to the sea over a considerable expanse all round the island, and which are doubtless identical with, or nearly allied to, those which cause the well-known vermilion sea off the coast of California.

[1] Journal of Friar Odoricus in the *Hakluyt Voyages*, vol. ii. p. 38.

CHAPTER VIII

FLORA

Such is the extraordinary wealth and variety of the Ceylon flora that a bare enumeration of the different trees, shrubs, plants, fruits, and flowers would fill many pages. All I shall attempt to do here is to make mention of such as everywhere strike the eye, giving a more extended description of those which are distinguished for use or beauty.[1]

Beginning with the larger trees, the one which above all others is identified with Ceylon is the Palm, a tree familiar to us as a symbol of triumph, and ever held in veneration from the earliest ages. Mohammed said of it that it was like a virtuous and generous man standing "erect before the Lord; in every action he follows the impulse

[1] The best account of the tropical flora will be found in Rhind's *History of the Vegetable Kingdom*.

received from above, and his whole life is devoted to the welfare of his fellow-creatures." There are several indigenous species in the island, including the Coco, Palmyra, Areca, Taliput, Doum, Kitool, Sago, and Date.

The queen of the whole tribe is without doubt the Taliput (*Corypha umbraculifera*) or Great Fan Palm, called by the natives *talagalia*, with a slender white stem and crown of fan-shaped leaves, a tree to which the Tamuls assign 801 different uses. This noble tree, which towers above its neighbours like a column of Carrara marble 100 feet high, blossoms but once between its fiftieth and eightieth year, the case or bud in which the flower is packed being 4 feet long, and bursting when ripe with a sharp cracking noise. The fans form a semicircle, each from 12 to 15 feet in radius, making a surface of something like 150 square feet. These, when cut into narrow strips, boiled and dried, form the *ola* or paper upon which are written the sacred Buddhist manuscripts in the Pali tongue, which for 2000 years has been a dead language. It is the younger sister of Sanskrit, their common mother being the long-lost Aryan. There is in the library of the Royal Asiatic Society a copy of a Pali book (*Pansyapanas Jatakaya*) written on 1172 laminæ of the finest taliput leaf, and containing the whole moral and religious code of Buddhism. I have handled many of these taliput manuscripts in the temples, for the most part in splendid preservation, with the writing still perfectly clear and distinct after the lapse of twenty centuries.

I was fortunate when going up to Kandy the first time to see no less than 40 taliput trees in full flower, each tall spike of bloom at least 30 feet high, and composed of myriads of small pale yellow blossoms. It is of this same taliput palm that Robert Knox writes: "It is as big and tall as a ship's mast and very straight, bearing only leaves which are of great use and benefit to this people, one single leaf being so broad and large that it will cover some fifteen or twenty men, and keep them dry when it rains. The leaf being dried is very strong and limber, and most wonderfully made for men's convenience to carry along with them, for though this leaf be thus broad when it is open, yet it will fold close like a lady's fan, and then it is no bigger than a man's arm; it is wonderfully light; they cut them into pieces and carry them in their hands. The whole leaf spread is round almost like a circle, but being cut in pieces for use are near like unto a triangle; they lay them upon their heads as they travel, with the peaked end foremost, which is convenient to make their way through the boughs and thickets. When the sun is vehement hot they use them to shade themselves from the heat; soldiers all carry them, for besides the benefit of keeping them dry in case it rain upon the march, these leaves make their tents to lie under in the night. A marvellous mercy which Almighty God hath bestowed upon this poor and naked people in this rainy country."

Hardly inferior in any respect is the Palmyra palm (*Borassus flabelliformis*), of which large numbers grow in the north and on the Jaffna peninsula. The stem is black and straight, thicker than the taliput, and crowned by a thick sheaf of stiff deep-cut pinnate leaves. This palm is said to live for 300 years like the elephant, but a more certain fact is that it produces the most esteemed kind of toddy.

Surpassing all others in usefulness, although of less conspicuous beauty than either the palmyra or the taliput, is the Coco palm, often erroneously spelt cocoa. Need I say that there is no connection between the product of this invaluable tree (*Cocos nucifera*) and that of *Theobroma cacao*, the common cocoa and chocolate of the breakfast table? The latter is the almond-like seed of a fruit something like a red and yellow cucumber, as unlike a coco-nut as possible. The coco proper gets its name either from the Greek *kokos*, meaning a seed or nut, or from a Portuguese word meaning a mask, to which the lower part of the nut is supposed to bear a resemblance. The coco palm is called by the natives *sayuga* or *polgaha*, and grows abundantly everywhere up to about 1500 feet above sea-level. It is a graceful feathery tree, growing usually to a height of from 60 to 80 feet; the stem is light-coloured, and made up of hard flexible black fibres united by a soft brown cellular substance capable of being reduced to powder. It has no analogy with the interior structure of any other tree, and most resembles in outward growth the white lily, which (although the plant is an annual) consists of a congeries of leaves rising one above another, each being joined at the base in an apparent stem. In habit palms are like ferns ; in blossom like grass ; in fructification like the asparagus tribe.

There are in Ceylon five varieties of the coco, all of which require an average temperature of 75° or 80°, and an annual rainfall of not less than 70 inches. It is said, like all palms, never to flourish away from the sound of the sea and the human voice ; but I have seen fine topes of palm at Kandy and Badoola, at an elevation of nearly 2000 feet and at least 100 miles from the sea. According to Mr. Ferguson, the well-known naturalist in Ceylon, there are about 25,000,000 coco trees in the island at the present time, growing on 628,344 acres, each tree producing on an average 80 nuts a year, with a yield of 10 quarts of oil. The proper time for planting the coco is just before the rains, when the soundest nuts are laid longitudinally, with one end slightly raised, in holes with a little salt, and lightly covered with 6 inches of earth. Each nut is placed so that the germ eye is presented towards the surface. On the eighteenth day or thereabouts, the germ appears above ground, white and smooth like the small tooth of an elephant, in which stage of its growth it is sometimes used as an expensive table delicacy roasted in ashes. After two years, during which it is carefully watered from time to time, it is transplanted, and bears no fruit until the tenth year, when the nuts appear in bunches of from eight to twelve, each containing about a dozen. As a young tree it needs a great deal of care and watchfulness, for among its foes are white ants, rats, parrots, porcupines, flying-foxes, and squirrels. It has no worse enemy than the coco beetle (*Batocera rubus*), a longicorn insect, whose large pulpy larvæ eat their way about recklessly in the stems of the young tree.

The uses of the coco are said to be as many as the days of the year, and a man with twelve cocos and two jak trees is considered independent. It supplies the people with food, drink, sugar, oil, wine, domestic utensils, building and thatching materials, clothes, cups, carpets, candles, coffins, cradles, mats, baskets, brushes, soap, spoons, paper, fans, fences, hats, hookahs, umbrellas, boats, ropes, sails, and many kinds of ornaments. As old George Herbert says—

The Indian nut alone
Is clothing, meat, and trencher, drink, and can,
Boat, cable, sail, mast, needle, all in one.

When a native has felled his palm, with its trunk he builds his hut and bullock-stall, which he thatches with the leaves. Slips of the bark form his bolts and bars; with the stalks he fertilises his little patch of chillies, tobacco, or grain. His baby swings to sleep in a coir net, and eats its rice and scraped nut boiled over a fire of nutshells, out of a dish of plaited leaves with a spoon made from the shell. The fisherman by torchlight carries a net made of the fibre; his torch is a bundle of leaves and flower-stalks; his fishing-boat is the stem. When thirsty he drinks the fresh juice, when hungry he eats the soft kernel. When he wants a stimulant he sips the arrack or the toddy, with the vinegar from which he flavours his curry. He dances to the tinkling of castanets made of the shell; he sweetens his coffee with jagery and dilutes it with coco milk. When he is sick his body is rubbed with the oil, which also feeds his shell lamp. Doors, windows, shelves, everything, from the water gutter to his child's money-box, is made from this wonderful tree. Over his couch when born, over his grave when buried, there hangs a bunch of coco blossom to scare away evil spirits. Its ground shell is used to adulterate cinnamon, cloves, pepper, ginger, nay, even coffee. It is a saying that he who plants a coco-nut leaves for his children house, raiment, and food.

The chief commercial products of the coco are: 1, OIL, from which are made stearine candles, and which is exported to the extent of 90,000 tons a year, worth 320 rupees a ton, fifty nuts yielding one gallon. 2, COIR, the fibre of the husk (from Tamul *kayaru*, meaning string), made into cables, which, although rougher than hempen ones, are very light and buoyant, and from their tannic properties stand exposure better than any others to the action of salt water. Their extreme elasticity makes them better adapted for running than for standing rigging. Upwards of 10,000 tons of coir are annually shipped from Colombo, worth ten rupees a ton. It is prepared by throwing the husks into brackish water, where they are left to ferment, after which the fibre is beaten free by women and children. 3, COPRA, or copperah, the dried kernel from which the oil is pressed. The export reaches 15,000 tons, worth seven or eight rupees a ton, each containing 6000 or 8000 nuts. The nuts are stored upon a raised stage under a shed and kept for three months or so, at the end of which time the water inside has dried up and the kernel is like leather. Often, however, they are dried much more quickly in the sun, being skinned, broken in half, the liquid thrown away and the kernels laid out in the open air: in three days they are ready for use. One coolie can pick, peel, and break 400 nuts a day. 4, POONAC, the oil-cake left after the extraction of the oil, useful as food for pigs. 5, TODDY, or *sura*, made also from the palmyra and kitool palms, by cutting off the ends of the flower-spikes just as they are ready to burst the sheath, the juice being allowed to run into an earthen pot. The Singhalese sometimes call toddy *mee-ra*, or sweet water; in Malaysia it is *aer-saguer*, for which the Hebrew is *shekar*, the "strong drink" of the Bible. Saint Jerome says that any strong drink, of corn, barley, or fruits, is called *shekar*, whence comes (through the Latin *sicera* or *sidera*) our English word *cyder*. 6, ARRACK is made from the distilled sap, and is generally used by the natives mixed with a bitter drug or hot pepper: pineapples steeped in arrack acquire a very delicious flavour. From the coco also is obtained the oleaginous fluid which forms the basis of curry (Singh. *cathy*, Malay *cari*). The Ceylon curry is light in colour and easily digested. The wood of the coco palm, with its black and white fibres, is known as "porcupine wood," and although inferior to that of the kitool or the palmyra, is much used for household purposes.

The Areca (*A. catechu*) or Pinang Palm is the most prolific of all, and is dear to the heart of the betel-eater, since it is from this tree that he procures the strong astringent nut, which he and his wife and children chew from morning to night. As the Chinaman must have his opium, the Fijian his *kava*, the Turkish belle her gum-mastic, the American his "quid," the Peruvian miner his *coca* leaf, so are the Singhalese inconsolable without the betel, which, according to a Sanskrit poem, possesses thirteen properties "not to be met with even in heaven." I have already described the process of chewing, and need only mention here that the areca palm grows with a straight delicate stem not more than 5 inches thick, and although a smaller tree than the coco, is more than twice as fruitful.

Next comes the Kitool (*Caryota urens*) or Jagery Palm, of which 30,000 acres are grown, chiefly for the sake of its sugary sap, from which is prepared jagery or palm-sugar, as well as toddy. The word jagery is from the Singhalese *sackarur*, the Sanskrit *segour*, English *sugar*, German *zucker*. Chunam or calcined lime used for building is mixed with jagery, for which the walls are prepared by a strong infusion of unripe coco husks called *lanias*. In appearance the kitool looks not unlike a gigantic hearse plume, with dark green leaves tinged with gray. The tree will yield 100 pints of sap in 24 hours. From the pith a sago is obtained, while fishing lines and bowstrings are made from the thin leaf fibres, the thicker parts of which are twisted into ropes used in elephant-hunting. The stem supplies the *pingo* or long flexible staff, upon which the coolies can carry a load of 80 pounds, the dead weight being much reduced by the springiness of the wood.

The Date Palm (*Phœnix dactylifera*) grows only 4 or 5 feet high in Ceylon, and bears a fruit containing 58 per cent of sugar. The fertilisation of this tree is aided by cutting off the male inflorescences just at the time of maturity, and hanging them among those of the female tree.

The Doum (*Hyphæne crinita*) is a variety of palm with a forked stem, each branch bearing a crown of fan-shaped leaves. In Ceylon it is, so far as I have noticed, a finer tree than in Arabia, its proper home, where I have seen it less luxuriant, with smaller leaves and less abundant fruit.

The only other palm I need mention is the Sago, from which the natives grind a flour much inferior to that of the taliput and other kinds.

A near relative of the palms is found in the order Pandanaceæ, of which the Pandanus (*P. odoratissimus*) or Screw Pine (more correctly Screw Palm) is the most distinguished member. Between the palms and screw pines a link is seen in *Phytelephas macrocarpa*, a native of South America, from the nut of which (*corozo*), the size of a hen's egg, is made the well-known vegetable ivory, largely used in Birmingham factories for buttons and trinkets. The pandanus, so called from a Malay word *pandang* meaning "conspicuous," grows to a height of 40 feet, with a stem forked like a candelabrum. Its dark green leaves are large and sword-shaped, with spiny edges and bases arranged in a close spiral form, from the bottom of which hang racemes of white or, as I have seen them in Fiji, yellow blossom. The aerial adventitious roots, the fibres of which are in request by basket-makers, grow like those of the fig and snake trees, and the amber clusters of fruit resembling a pineapple are eaten by the natives. Inside are found a number of nearly square red capsules, smooth as ivory; these are chewed, and the *kilo* or kernel is extracted looking like a filbert. This when grated resembles dark brown sawdust, which is moistened, kneaded, and baked. In the peculiar growth of the roots we see a careful provision of nature for the support of the enormous top-weight of thick fleshy leaves, by which the tree would lose its balance but for the aid thus afforded. The juicy branches when cut up are greatly relished by cattle, and from the blossoms is made a much-esteemed perfume.

Hard by the temples is often found the Banyan (*Ficus Indica*), first cousin of the Bo-tree, *bo-gaha*, pipal or peepul, one of the Artocarpaceæ, a tree of which Strabo gives an accurate description. It presents a singular appearance, with its huge pendent aerial roots fantastically twisted, between which are found numbers of Gothic-like arches supporting a canopy of branches. When the boughs have extended about 12 feet laterally, they shoot down towards the earth and there take root; when matured they propagate inwards in the same manner, until the whole becomes like a tent supported by many columns. There is a banyan in the south of India which is said to cast at noon a shadow 1116 feet in circumference. The fruit is like a hazel nut and useless. Southey's description of the banyan tree in "The Curse of Kehama" is very fine and true to nature:—

It was a goodly sight to see
That venerable tree,
For o'er the lawn, irregularly spread,
Fifty straight columns propt its lofty head;
And many a long depending shoot
Seeking to strike its root
Straight like a plummet grew towards the ground.
Some on the lower boughs which crost their way,
Fixing their bearded fibres, round and round,
With many a ring and wild contortion wound;
Some to the passing wind at times with sway
Of gentle motion swung;
Others of younger growth unmov'd were hung
Like stone-drops from the cavern's fretted height.

Growing somewhat in the same fashion are the evergreen Mangroves, a root-throwing clan, of which the commonest is *Rhizophora mangle*; all are alike in the thick stems, which rise from the middle of a clump of many-branched roots growing out of the water to a height of 10 or 12 feet, and offering a retreat to vast numbers of birds and crabs. Oysters sometimes cling to the boughs, which gave rise to the fable of oyster-bearing trees seen by early navigators in the east.

A noble forest tree is the Tamarind (*T. Indica*) or Indian date, called by the Singhalese *seyembala*, of gigantic proportions, with crooked boughs, acacia-like leaf, and strongly aromatic straw-yellow blossoms with red-veined petals, growing in loose bunches of five or six from the sides of the branches. The tree is too valuable to be much used for its excessively hard wood, of a fine dark red marked with black. The dark reddish purple of the flower pod, twice as long as in the West Indies, when mixed with hot water and a squeeze of lime and sugar, makes a refreshing drink, sharp but not unpleasantly acid, and of a refrigerant laxative nature. The tree is called in Arabic *tamar hinde*. Marco Polo in describing the kingdom of Gozurat informs us that "the people are the most desperate pirates in existence, and one of their most atrocious practices is this. When they have taken a merchant vessel they force the merchant to swallow a stuff called Tamarinds mixed in sea-water, which produces a violent purging. This is done in case the merchants, on seeing their danger, should have swallowed their most valuable stones and pearls."

The Bread-fruit tree (*Artocarpus incisa*) grows to the size of a tall oak, with deep green leaves and rather soft wood. It is during eight months in the year such a prolific bearer that two of them will suffice for a man's maintenance. Dr. Solander, who accompanied Captain Cook in his South Sea voyages, called it "the most useful vegetable in the world." It is of the bread-fruit that Lord Byron sings—

> *The bread-tree, which without the ploughshare yields*
> *The unreaped harvest of unfurrowed fields,*
> *And bakes its unadulterated loaves*
> *Without a furnace in unpurchased groves,*
> *And flings off famine from its fertile breast,*
> *A priceless market for the gathering guest.*

The fruit is heart-shaped with a thick outer rind, and when baked is like wheaten bread-crumb, but less palatable.

Of the same family and growing round every hamlet is the Jak (*A. integrifolia*), the Singhalese *kos-gass*, the Indian *jaka*, the wood of which, like coarse mahogany, takes a fine polish, and is much used for cheap furniture; when freshly cut it is yellow, but deepens with age. The fruit, one of which often weighs half a hundredweight, and two of which slung on a *pingo* make a good load for a strong coolie, consists of a fleshy pulp, the possible pleasantness of which is discounted by an intensely nasty odour, which I can compare only to the top-end of a London omnibus on a very warm wet day. In the centre of the pulp lies a nut, which is not bad eating when roasted. This variety of *artocarpus* gets its name *integrifolia* from its leaf being entire in shape, whereas that of the bread-tree is deeply gashed (*incisa*). It was in search of this last-named tree that the *Bounty* was despatched to the South Seas upon the voyage in which the famous mutiny took place.

The Del (*A. nobilis*) is a finely-growing tree, useful for making canoes. The fruit is as large as a water-melon, and has a tough juice used as bird-lime.

In some districts, especially in the north and

east, many noble Teaks (*Tectona grandis*), called by the Malabars *tekka*, are found, from whose leaves is expressed a purple dye. It is a straight-growing tree, which in maturity tops all its neighbours, often rising to a height of 200 feet. It has panicles of snowy flowers, and deciduous leaves 20 inches long, like an elephant's ear, and covered with rough points; when freshly cut the timber, which abounds in particles of silex, smells like a rose.

The fragrant Champac (*Michelia C.*) is one of the magnolias, getting its botanic name from P. A. Micheli, a famous Florentine microscopical botanist. It is often called the moon-flower, from the fact that it opens only at night its pale yellow blossoms.

Of the Plumieria genus there are several Ceylon species, among them being *P. acuminata* and *P. acutifolia*, or temple-tree, a large shrub-tree, an exotic from South America, with a curious crooked stem and almost leafless straggling boughs, swelling out at the ends, on which there are a number of small strongly-scented red and yellow blossoms, used as offerings in the temples. For the same purpose are used also the Jasmine (*J. grandiflorum* and *J. sambac*), the Persian *yasmin* and Arabic *ysmyn*, and the Oleander (*Nerium odoratum*), with its blossoms far finer even than the superb ones of Spain and South Italy. This plant, although little suspected, contains a formidable poison, which forms the basis of several remedies in use for cutaneous maladies, and as vermin poison. It is upon a plant of the same order (*Apocynaceæ* or dogbanes) that the Singhalese say Eve found the forbidden fruit, which still bears the marks of her teeth, and has ever since been poisonous.

Standing in among palms and jaks are to be seen the stately Mango, the gorgeous Silk-cotton, and the picturesque Pisang, better known as the Banana or fig of paradise. Of these the Silk-cotton (*Bombax malabaricus*) or *Salmalia* is the most attractive to the eye, and is called by the Singhalese *kattoo-imbul*. It is a thorny tree with bright green stem, and puts forth its crimson flowers before the tulip-like leaves. In due course appear the pods, in which lie black shiny seeds embedded in a kind of floss used for pillow-stuffing. The Mango (*Mangifera Indica*) bears twice a year a crop of tough green (and very perishable) fruit looking like a short thick cucumber the size of a goose egg, containing a luscious and slightly acid pulp, which melts in the mouth with refreshing coolness, and when unripe makes a very excellent pickle. The best grow near Jaffna in the north, and are in Ceylon pretty much what the apple is in England, with a flavour not to be imagined by those who have only tasted it in pickle. The dense shining leathery leaves, 8 inches long, make a most grateful shade, and have a sweet resinous odour; the small blossoms in bunches at the end of the boughs are pinky white.

Familiar as the fruit of the banana and plantain (*Musa paradisaica, M. sapientum*) is now in the London market, few persons can have any idea of the beauty of the tree when growing in the tropics. Everywhere in Ceylon on the lower lands are to be seen the elegant sheaves of gigantic drooping pale green leaves, which are often used for thatch. There is a certain disordered *abandon* and unkempt look about the banana, which is caused by the splitting and jagging of its foliage by the wind. There are at least five varieties to be seen any day in the Colombo market: 1, Lady's finger banana, sweet, small, and golden, most delicious of all. 2, Water banana, large, and with cool juicy flesh like a cucumber. 3, Potato banana, solid, mealy, and floury. 4, Pineapple banana, with a delicate aroma. 5, Cinnamon banana, with a spicy flavour, and excellent (as indeed are all the others) boiled or baked, made into fritters, or eaten raw with cheese. Enormous quantities of this fruit are consumed, its nutritious properties being far in excess of any other known vegetable food. Humboldt states that as a food-producer the banana is to the potato as 44, and to wheat as 133, to 1. From the stem of the tree is expressed a juice which when fermented makes a pleasant wine, while the tops of the young plants make a delicate vegetable.

The Ironwood tree (*Mesua ferrea*) is found near many of the temples, and is called by the natives *na-gass*. Its rose-like flowers with ivory-white petals and orange-coloured stamens, in charming contrast with the deep crimson buds and shoots, are often used as floral offerings. It gets its botanical name from Meuse, an Arabian botanist of the eighth century. Sir William Jones called this tree "one of the most beautiful on earth." The dried blossom known as *nagkesur* is sold in every Indian bazaar. It is this noble tree of which Thomas Moore sings—

> *Those sweet flow'rets that unfold*
> *Their buds on Kamadeva's quiver,*

in allusion to a Hindoo belief that their god Cupid tips his darts with the blossom.

The Tulip tree (*Liriodendron tulipifera*) grows mostly near the sea, with fine yellow blossoms and hard heavy tough wood, much used for gun-stocks and by London coach-builders for the panels of carriages. Linnæus calls the tree *Hibiscus populneus*, because it has the leaf of the poplar and the flower of the hibiscus. It is the same tree, I believe, that is known in the United States as poplar or whitewood.

The Satin (*Chloroxylon Swieteniæ*), the native *booroota*, is a truly noble forest tree, far more imposing than in India, with a gray bark, small white blossoms, and a wood useful for building purposes. In the east near Trincomalee many of them grow to a height of 100 feet.

No less majestic and much less common is the Calamander (*Diospyros hirsuta, D. quæsita*), the native *kalu medereya*, which surpasses all other fancy woods in the beauty of its timber. It is like the finest rosewood, rich brown mottled with black, dense and hard, and taking a polish like glass. It is a rare variety of the better known Ebony (*D. ebenus*), of which there are extensive forests in the north. The ebony has a sooty trunk that looks as if it had been charred; under the bark the wood is white as far as the heart, whence comes the well-known timber. The fruit, which contains 60 per cent of pure tannic acid, is eaten by natives only, who also use the juice as a hardener for canoes, cords, nets, etc.

The Camphor tree (*Dryabalanops C.*) does not appear to grow to such proportions as in Java and Sumatra, where it is often found 200 feet high and 7 or 8 feet thick. It was in old times looked upon as the tallest tree in the world, before the discovery of the Australian and Californian giants. The precious consolidated camphor is found in crystalline masses in fissure-like hollows in the trunk, in quantities varying from a quarter of a pound to a pound in each tree; the oil is obtained by bruising and boiling the twigs. Marco Polo says that in his day the Malay camphor was worth "its weight in fine gold." To this day it sells among the Chinese for its weight in silver, being a hundred times as valuable as that found in China, where it is called *ping-pieu* or "icicle-flakes." Although the earliest kind of camphor known, it is not now exported to Europe, the ordinary camphor of commerce being the product of *Cinnamomum camphora.*

The Coral (*Erythrina Indica*) with a thorny stem sends forth superb flowers, like the silk-cotton, before the leaves. Of Oranges and Lemons there is no lack; and equally common is the Ipecacuanha (*I. cephaelis,* from Greek *cephale,* a head, because its leaves are disposed in heads), a native of Brazil, with a bright orange flower. Acacia (*A. concinna*), with brilliant flaming plumes, and *A. Arabica,* with a bark used in tanning and esteemed as a tonic, are found side by side with *Hibiscus Zeylanica,* or Shoe-plant, a fine mallow with large yellow flowers, and *H. rosa sinensis,* with red.

Among trees less known are the curious fan-shaped Traveller's tree, which gets its name of *Urania speciosa* from the Greek *ouranos,* meaning "sublime"; it grows something like the banana, with leaves useful for thatching, the stalk containing even in drought about a quart of pure and pleasant liquid : the handsome Moorooto (*Lagerstrœmia reginæ*, from a Swedish botanist), with beautiful pale rose blossoms deepening to purple; the Halmileel or Halmilla (*Berrya amornilla*), called sometimes Trincomalee wood, valuable for cask staves, and growing with a straight stem to a height of 40 feet; from it are made the Madras surf boats : the Mustard (*Salvadoria Persica*), the mustard tree of the Bible; the Ceylon oak (*Schleicheia trijuga*), the Singhalese *koang*, from the burnt acorns of which comes a useful oil; the evergreen Yucca (*Y. gloriosa*) or Adam's needle, introduced from Persia; and *Sterculia fœtida*, the native *goorœnda*, with a revolting smell of rotten flesh, an object of aversion to natives and travellers alike. In the giant Casuarina (*C. equisetifolia*) we have a link with the flora of Australia, its thirty species being found in that country and Ceylon alone, and its name derived from the cassowary bird (found in Queensland and the northern part of South Australia), to whose feathers the leaves are supposed to bear a resemblance.

Nor must we forget the crimson Rhododendron

(*R. nobile*), called by the natives *maha-rat-mal* or "great red flower," which with a girth of 3 or 4 feet takes rank as a timber tree, and grows to the height of 50 feet, to within a short distance of the top of Adam's Peak. The leaves make a pleasant jelly and the Singhalese eat the flower. One variety peculiar to the island has a leaf silvered upon the under side.

Surpassing in size some of the large trees are clumps of Bamboo (*Bambusa arundinacea*), in reality a giant grass. It is not used in Ceylon as it is in Malaysia, where the natives cut holes in the stalk through which the wind sighs, and to which they give the name of *bulu perindu* or plaintive bamboo.[1] Its value is scarcely inferior to that of the palm, with which it shares among Eastern peoples the honour of forming the staff of life. Scaffolding and ladders, landing jetties and fishing apparatus, scoops and irrigative wheels, oars, masts, and yards, sails, cables, and caulking, spears, arrows, bows, bowstrings, and quivers, paper, mats, torches, footballs, bellows, musical instruments, trays, boxes, conduits, cans and cooking-pots, hats, helmets, pickles, medicine,

[1] Note U.

and asparagus—these are some of the many uses of this grass, without which a native cannot imagine existence in any land to be possible.

Growing everywhere in the jungles are cactus-like Euphorbias (*Excæcaria agallocha*, etc.), with their leafless angular blue-green stems and acrid juice; Caladiums (*Colocasia antiquorum* and *C. odorata*), with great arrow-shaped leaves exquisitely tinted and spotted with red, useful as sunshades; Manihots (*M. janipha*), from Brazil, with a useful farina in the root; Vines and Lianas of a hundred varieties hanging in graceful festoons like artificially woven wreaths, or soaring to the tops of the tallest trees, gay with crimson or blue or golden flowers.

Coming back to trees properly so called, I must say a word about the Cinnamon (*C. Zeylanicum*), a member of the laurel tribe, and therefore first cousin to the coffee tree, called by Baldæus "the Helen or Bride in Contest of this Isle." It is now grown on some 36,000 acres, from which last year upwards of 2,000,000 pounds were exported. Although Galen spoke of cinnamon as a "present fit for kings," it is never by ancient writers connected specially with Ceylon. Kazwini in A.D.

1275 was the first to do so. We have no native records of the trade until A.D. 1406, when the *chalias* or cinnamon cutters were organised by the king to furnish him with a yearly supply. I have found the following account of the tree in the "Voyage and travel of M. Cæsar Fredericke, merchant of Venice A.D. 1563": "In this Iland," he says, "there groweth fine Sinamom, great store of Pepper, great store of Nuttes and Arochoe: there they make great store of Cairo [coir] to make Cordage: it bringeth foorth great store of Christall Cats' eyes, or *Ochi de Gati*, and they say that they finde there some Rubies. I was desirous to see how they gather the Sinamom, or take it from the tree that it groweth on, and so much the rather, because the time that I was there, was the season which they gather it in, which was in the moneth of Aprill, at which time the Portugals were in armes and in the field, with the king of the countrey; yet I to satisfie my desire, although in great danger, tooke a guide with mee and went into a wood three miles from the Citie, in which wood was great store of Sinamome trees growing together among other wilde trees; and this Sinamome tree is a small tree, and not very high, and hath leaves like to our Baie tree. In the moneth of March or Aprill, when the sappe goeth up to the toppe of the tree, then they take the Sinamom from that tree in this wise. They cut the barke of the tree round about in length from knot to knot, or from joint to joint, above and belowe, and then easilie with their handes they take it away, laying it in the sunne to drie. And yet for all this the tree dieth not, but agaynst the next yeere it will have a new barke." The operation is much the same at the present time. At the proper season the shoots or sticks are cut and peeled by men called *chalias*, whose sole work it is, and who idle away their days until the next season comes round. From the leaves clove oil is produced. In Dutch times the cinnamon-peeling was a feudal service to native princes, who had to pay to the Europeans an annual tribute of the prepared spice. Naturally the tree grows to a height of 40 feet, but it is usually pruned down to 10. It delights in a snow-white sandy quartz soil where little else will grow, and bears a soft blue fruit as big as an olive with a nut inside. From the fragments of the bark is made the costly oil of cinnamon, one ounce of which is produced by about 12 pounds' weight.

The Nutmeg tree (*Myristica moschata*) grows to 30 feet, and bears fruit like a small pointed peach with a thick coat. When ripe this bursts and yields (1) mace, which looks like a red leafy network surrounding the (2) nutmeg, larger and harder than a filbert, which is dried either in the sun or over a fire until the kernel rattles, when it is broken.

The Bhel or Bael tree (*Æglé marmelos*) is common near the sea in the south, and bears a delicious astringent fruit: root, bark, and leaves are all used medicinally; from the rind a perfume is prepared, and a cement from the seed.

The Mee (*Bassia longifolia*), a native of Sumatra, is a graceful tree growing 20 feet high, with a blossom like a single rose, and supplies the natives with a good building wood, as well as with an oil for their lamps. A variety of it is the *moonemal* (*Mimusops elengi*), very handsome in its growth, with dark leaves and fragrant white flowers. *Cassia fistula* is also a fine tree not unlike an ash, with gold pendent flowers 2½ feet long like the laburnum. Its black seed-pods 2 or 3 feet long look just like a crop of ebony rulers.

Camboge or Gamboge (*Garcinia morella*), called sometimes *Hebradendron combogioides*, the native *ghorka*, is the size of a small apple tree; the fruit, which is exceedingly acid, is dried and used in curry. From the bark is procured a gum resin, the source of the well-known colour. The acid exudation forms a strong purgative, and is used as the basis of a widely advertised popular pill.

A useful tree is the Sack tree or *rita-gaha*, the branches of which are cut into lengths from which the bark is beaten away; it is then bleached, and with one end sewn up makes a capital sack, which will last almost for ever.

From the exotic Betel (*Piper betel*) comes, as I have already said, the leaf dear to Singhalese and Tamuls alike. That the use to which it is universally put is not the outcome of modern dissipation is clear from the fact that the *Mahawanso*[1] mentions a princess, five centuries before the Christian era, who sent some of its leaves to her lover. Marco Polo tells us that in India all the people had "a custom of perpetually keeping in the mouth a certain leaf called *tembul* [Persian

[1] See *supra*, p. 23.

for betel-leaf], to gratify a certain habit and desire they have, continually chewing it and spitting out the saliva that it excites. The lords and gentlefolk and the King have these leaves prepared with camphor and other aromatic spices, and also mixt with quicklime. And this practice was said to be very good for the health. If any one desires to offer a gross insult to another, when he meets him he spits this leaf or its juice in his face." Garcias de Horta says: "In chewing *betre* they mix areca with it and a little lime; some add *liçio* (catechu), but the rich and grandees add some Borneo camphor, and some also lign-aloes, musk, and ambergris." Another writer tells us that "the manner of eating it is as follows: they bruise a portion of *faufel* (areca) and put it in the mouth; moistening a leaf of the betel, together with a grain of lime, they rub the one on the other, roll them together, and then place them in the mouth. They thus take as many as four leaves of betel at a time and chew them; sometimes they add camphor to it." All native races have a horror of white teeth, a disfigurement which they do their best to obliterate by the use of betel and areca. It is possible that a natural craving may underlie the practice, inasmuch as, since their diet of rice and fruit is an insipid and acid one, the betel may serve as an antiseptic, correcting acidity and acting as a tonic. In former times the Portuguese at Goa became so fond of betel that their women used to chew it even in bed.

For many years Coffee was the great "stand-by" of Ceylon. As far back as 1824 it was planted in the Gampola district on the site of an old Kandyan royal city. There were other plantations at Orowa Ganga and Matelle, but they never really flourished, owing in part to the heavy protective duties then levied in favour of the West India colonies. At the present time, now that its culture and preparation are better understood, coffee has been revived in these same districts with greater success. From 1850 onwards an immense impetus was given to the cultivation. Scores of planters and speculators, who bought large blocks of land at 5s. an acre, were attracted to the island, in many cases only to find ruin instead of riches. Everybody dabbled in coffee more or less—civil servants, government agents, the bar, the bench, and the Church, up to the Colonial Secretary and the Governor himself.

In those good times, with the same certainty as the seasons, the topped trees used to make their new wood, blossom in March and bear their cherries in the autumn; all seemed to promise well, and a few did actually realise the fortunes they looked for. Coolies were plentiful, and both soil and climate were apparently just what was wanted. But Dame Nature showed herself before long a capricious mistress; possibly she had been wooed with too much ardour. Whether the soil became prematurely exhausted, or whether the epidemic that smote the trees arose from causes beyond human control, we know not, and never shall know. In 1869, just as the export realised 1,000,000 hundredweight, appeared the leaf-fungus (*Hemileia vastatrix*), followed closely by the so-called "coffee-bug," which is in reality one of the diptera, a species of coccus (*Lecanium coffeæ*) covering the shoots with encrusted scales holding the larvæ, and attracted possibly by the weakness of the roots caused by the leaf disease. In frightful succession one estate after another was ruined; planter after planter "went under";

science and skill were baffled. In 1877 there were a quarter of a million acres under coffee; in 1887 not 100,000, and the area still decreasing. In twelve years the export fell from 1,000,000 hundredweight to 180,429.

In despair the gallant planters looked elsewhere for a substitute. Cocoa, cocaine, cinchona, were all tried, but the tide did not turn until it was discovered that Ceylon possesses perhaps the finest climate and soil in the world for the growth of Tea. The order went forth, "Exeat coffee, enter tea." Before 1870 there were not 350 acres growing tea; in 1890 there were 200,000, from which 23,820,471 pounds were shipped over sea mostly to London. We need not be surprised therefore that during the last few years the export of China tea to England has fallen off by 50,000,000 pounds. There is an immense and ever-growing demand for the Ceylon leaf, and the hearts of many who were sorely smitten by the coffee failure are made glad, as year after year they see worthless coffee estates turned into flourishing gardens, producing a tea which is most delicious, owing its special aromatic and pungent flavour doubtless to the strongly ferruginous soil. Of course there are croakers and prophets of woe, who predict a repetition of past disaster; it is possible that experience tends to show that large areas devoted exclusively year after year to any one cultivation are conducive to, or at least liable to, disease. But the fact remains that up to the present moment the tea has been wholly exempt from drawbacks, and free from those ravaging blights which in India often reduce the crop by one-half the average. It does not therefore seem rash to affirm, what all, indeed, must hope who have any knowledge of the gallant struggles and terrible losses of the old coffee planters, that the tea shrub, which, be it remembered, is grown not for the fruit but the leaf, has found in the island a congenial and permanent home, and that Ceylon will take and keep its place as the tea country of the world. It possesses peculiar advantages: (1) a convenient position for export and import of the "plant" used in the drying and packing of the crop; (2) a constant equatorial sun with regular monsoon rains, ensuring frequent flushes of new leaves; and (3) abundance of cheap labour.

In old times the clearing of a coffee estate was an imposing spectacle. It was no easy task to clear 100 or 1000 acres of Ceylon forest and undergrowing jungle; in fact there was only one way of doing it satisfactorily, and that was by fire. A gang of coolies working from the bottom to the top of a hillside cut through nine-tenths of each tree stem, each being left standing by a small portion of wood upon the lower side. Then when the word was given the topmost trees were felled, and in their fall brought down with a crash all below them. The timber, after lying for some weeks to dry, was then set on fire, and made a magnificent sight as one huge forest king after another was wrapped in flame.

The coffee-tree (*Jasminum Arabicum*) is a luxuriant evergreen shrub, growing pyramidally like a laurel, with handsome dark glistering lanceolate leaves, and is kept topped upon the higher lands at a growth of about 5 feet, which in the lower districts is increased to 20. The work of cultivation is carried on by Tamul coolies, who get from eightpence to a shilling a day, working from six to four. They are under no indentures, and can quit service at a month's notice. The trees, which are planted in rows 6 feet apart, are covered in March with fragrant white blossoms, followed by fruit first yellow and then purple-red, technically called cherries, from their close likeness to the red Kentish cherry. In September the regular picking season begins, and lasts for two or three months, although I have seen cherries here and there on the trees all the year round. The beans, of which a coolie can pick a couple of bushels a day, are enclosed in a "pulp," a kind of fleshy covering sweet to the taste, but of no use except as a fertiliser in a state of decomposition. The bean is passed through a pulper with cylindrical copper graters, which tear the flesh away from the cherry and leave the coffee in an inner covering called "parchment." It is then partially fermented by being left in heaps for some hours, after which the fleshy particles are loosened and detached in running water. The bean is then dried, usually in the sun, and packed in bags for sending to the Colombo rolling mills, where the parchment and under silver skin are detached, and the gray-blue berry is left ready for market and shipment.

As for the tea, the leaves when picked are placed in shallow baskets and left to stand in the sun for some hours, after which they are stirred about in iron pans over a charcoal stove. They are then carefully rubbed in the hands, and subjected to a lower temperature, the heat being just enough to dry without scorching them, after which they are laid out upon tables and picked over, the finer sorts being rolled up separately leaf by leaf.

In among the rows of the coffee or tea the Cinchona (order *Rubiaceæ*) has been increasingly grown for some years. It has a straight, slender, hard, close-grained stem, and bears a white flower, with leaves a glorious red when young. The bark, which is skinned off with a keen knife, is exported to the extent of 12,000,000 or 13,000,000 pounds a year, a supply likely to prove in excess of the demand, seeing that if the alkaloids are taken at only 4 per cent, this means a production of 6,000,000 ounces of the febrifuge. It seems open to question whether the cinchona will continue to flourish in a soil which, from its nature, is so well suited to tea.

Next to coffee and tea we must rank Rice (*Oryza sativa*) as among the most valuable products of Ceylon. The 800,000 acres of rice require great and constant labour. Before the grain comes to maturity it has to run the gauntlet of foes innumerable: hogs, birds, elephants, are all against it; sometimes just when most needed the water-supply will fail, or the dam will be broken down by wild animals. Fires have often to be kept burning in the watch-houses; an army of children must be perpetually pulling the long lines attached to the bird-rattles; wind-clackers must be kept going. Enormous as is the rain-fall in Ceylon, it is not enough for the rice: artificial irrigation is the first essential; a perfectly level bed or succession of levels is the second. After being well watered and reduced to mud, the land is ploughed to a depth of 18 inches, and the water again turned on until the ground is soft enough to take a man in up to his knees. Then gangs of buffalo are driven in to trample it about until the water has disappeared, and a perfectly level surface is left upon which the soaked *padi* is sown. In a fortnight it will grow to a height of 4 inches. The padi fields often present a pretty sight, some of the hills being cut from top to bottom in terraces covered with the brilliant green plant.

Sago, so called from *Sagu*, meal (*Metroxylon*

Rumphii), is procured from several trees, as well as from the taliput palm. The tree is cut into lengths and split, after which the pith is dug out, chopped up, and washed repeatedly through sieves until all the starch has disappeared. The water of the washings is then collected and left to stand until the starch in it settles. When dried this is fit for use in calico factories, etc. The sago as used for food is in a granulated form, and is half baked, for which reason it will keep good for a long time.

The finest quality of Arrowroot (*Maranta arundinacea, M. Malaccensis*) is obtained from a pretty orchidaceous plant 2 feet high, common on the patanas or grass-lands, the savannahs of Ceylon. *M. Indica* on the mainland sells for its weight in rupees. The plant, which has light green deeply indented leaves, gets its name from the tiny shaft or stalk, on the end of which the pink flower grows like a hyacinth, with a delightful perfume. When the leaves show signs of decay the small bulbous root, as thick as a finger, is dug up, freed from its scaly covering, mashed to a pulp, and when dried in the sun is ready for market.

Sugar (*Saccharum officinarum*) was first made in 1837 at Dumbara, but ten years were enough to show that it would pay no better than cotton, indigo, hemp, and tobacco. These are indeed grown to some extent, but with little effect in a soil that is too poor to bring any of them to their best. I believe that at the present time but one sugar estate is worth having, and that is at Peredeniya. Ceylon sugar is a dull gray colour and very moist, needing much lime in order to crystallise it: the straw-coloured sugar grown in a dry and stiff rich soil can never be produced. Cocos and cinnamon are the only products that really do well in the island without any artificial fertilisation whatever.

Indigo (*Indigofera tinctoria*) is a veritable "child of the sun," flourishing in a moderately moist temperature of not less than 70°. The plant, 2 feet high, is reaped with sickles as soon as it flowers, the stalks being cut (three or four times a year) close to the ground. The whole plant is used for dyeing purposes, the dye being extracted by fermentation. The branches are placed stem upwards in a vat until it is three parts full, when they are covered with water. Fermentation goes on until in 24 hours the contents of the vat are so hot that the hand cannot be held in it. The liquor is then drawn off and stirred about in another cistern, after which the indigo separates in flakes: lime water is added and the blue allowed to subside, the water being then drawn off and the sediment pressed and cut into small squares. In America the dye is obtained by scalding, but the product is inferior. An acre of indigo plants will yield 400 or 500 pounds weight of the dye, worth about 10 shillings a pound. The French call the plant *anil*, the Arabs *nile*; in Portugal and South America it is *nil*: the English word is a manifest corruption of *indicum*.

In Wild Plants of great variety, of which I can mention but a few, Ceylon is very rich. The Lotus (*Nymphæa L.*), both pink and white, is of great beauty and a common ornament of the tanks and sluggish streams. The leaf is larger than that of a water lily, and the flower as large again, with a seed about the size of a hazel nut, often taken by the natives as a mild narcotic. The Arabs call the fruit *nuphar*, under which name when dried it is often sold as a sponge.

The Brahmans say that once upon a time a self-existent Being hatched an egg (who laid it deponent sayeth not) upon a lotus leaf that was floating upon the water, and that out of the egg came the world. The Buddhists reject this tale inasmuch as they believe in no creative act whatever.

The Devil's Apple (*Datura stramonium*) possesses also certain narcotic properties, but is used only as a medicine. It grows like a weed all over the island, as does also the Castor-oil plant (*Ricinus communis*).

The Indian Hemp (*Crotalaria juncea*) is identical with the *haschisch* of the Egyptians, and is used in the preparation of the stimulating *bhang*, called by the Arabians "the cementer of friendship and increaser of pleasures," and supposed to be the *nepenthes* of Homer. The leaves and flowers are dried and made into a paste, which is chewed with a sensation of dreamy happiness, followed by a slight depression, soon rectified by a sip of arrack. The fibres of one variety (*Sanseviera Zeylanica*) are used for cordage, nets, etc.

Mustard (*Sinapis ramosa*) grows freely, as does

Pepper (*P. nigrum*). Wild Ginger (*Amonum zingiber*) is abundant, its rather tasteless root being a favourite food of elephants, which seem, strangely enough, to despise the succulent leaves. The cultivated variety (*Z. officinale*) is also common. According to an old writer named Pegolotti, "the *Colombino* ginger (*gigembre Columbin*) grows in the island of Colombo, and has a smooth, delicate, ash-coloured rind." It appears among the purchases made for King John of France during his captivity in England, the price paid being thirteenpence a pound, equal now to about four shillings and fourpence.

Gourds are plentiful and various. The Calabash (Portuguese *calabaça*) or Bottle-gourd (*Cucurbita lagenaria*), different from *Crescentia cujete* of the West Indies, is so called from its shape and the use to which it is put, the tough hard rind being used for bowls, etc.

The best Fruits in Ceylon are not, with one or two exceptions, the indigenous ones.[1] Pineapples (*Bromelia*) are plentiful and fine, although lacking, to my taste, the flavour of the best English hot-

[1] Note V.

house ones. The Mangostan or mangosteen (*Garcinia mangostana*), a delicious fruit, was introduced from Sumatra. It is round and the size of an orange, with a queer little cap on the top, a brown shell like a pomegranate, interior divisions like an orange, and a taste like mixed strawberry and grape.

Cherry and Peach trees grow in the hills, where they become evergreens, with fruit that never reaches perfection.

The Durian (*Durio zibethinus*), which I once tried to eat in Fiji, cannot be classed among the island fruits, but is worthy of mention among tropical products as far and away the very nastiest thing in the vegetable kingdom. The historic *stchi* of Russia, consisting of beef broth and cabbage "seasoned" with sour cream; the *gamle ost* of Norway, a cheese that has a flavour like old brown Windsor soap, and a smell that you can cut with a knife; the Spanish delicacy called *mangia blanca* of poultry and vinegar; the raw turtle egg of the tropics; these all are nasty, but they are as nothing to a durian. Yet I have met people who said they liked it: to me the smell even in memory is absolutely revolting. The fruit is the size of a man's head, and looks something like the bread-fruit, with a hard warty rind. Inside is a thick creamy pulp, tasting like rotten meat and vegetables.

The Papaw (*Carica papaya*) has a tall hollow stem with yellow fruit like a small melon, containing round black seeds, and is delicious eaten with sugar and pepper: unripe in a pickled state it is as good as mango. The natives use the leaves instead of soap for washing clothes. The juice and sap have the curious property of making the toughest meat tender: it is a common sight to see pieces hung up among the boughs.

The Jambu or Malay apple (*J. Zeylanica, Eugenia Malaccensis*) is white and waxy, with a poor flavour of rose-leaves, from which it is often called "rose-apple," a name rightly belonging to a smaller and rarer fruit (*E. jambos*), which grows on a tree 20 or 30 feet high, with long narrow peach-like leaves: the fruit is as big as a hen's egg and tastes like an apricot.

The Loquat (*Eriobotrya Japonica*) is like a very small round apple, the colour of an apricot, and with a pleasantly acid taste.

The Shaddock (so called from Captain Shaddock, who first brought it from China) or *poncolo* (*Citrus decumana*) is a cross between an orange and a lemon, not found wild; a finer fruit here than in the West Indies.

There are fair Grapes at Jaffna in the north, but as a rule the absence of all winter in the island prevents them from coming to great excellence.

The Litchi (*Dimocarpus L.*), a well-known Chinese species of plum, is found abundantly, growing in clusters, each the size of a walnut, with their red scaly coat and pleasant sweet pulp.

The Custard-apple or Sweet-sop (*Anona muricata, A. squamosa*), a native of the West Indies, in appearance resembles an artichoke, but is larger and flatter, with a thick yellow rind, under which is a creamy custard-like yellow pulp, very sweet and luscious. I had heard so much about this fruit before I tasted it for the first time that I think it did not come up to my expectations. Pomegranates are abundant but not indigenous, having been introduced by the Portuguese. The Guava (*Psidium*) is like a hen's egg but yellow, with red seedy pulp and a taste not unlike that of a strawberry.

A curious fruit is the Cashew nut (*Anacardium*

occidentale), a perfect freak of nature. The kernel grows outside instead of in, the fruit and nut being joined at the end but otherwise distinct. It is yellow like an Eve-apple and nasty in taste, with a juice used for soldering metals. The Dutch used to make a strong liqueur from it, although the oil is a very poisonous one, and sometimes used by the natives for evil purposes.

The *katum-billé*, a red, rough-skinned, stoneless wild plum, is the size of a greengage and has an acid taste; in the form of jelly it makes a good substitute for marmalade. At Nuwara Eliya there are capital blackberries and passable raspberries. Cape gooseberries (*solanum*) are like yellow cherries covered with a loose outer skin; they are sour but aromatic, and by no means to be despised either in a raw or preserved state. The Granadilla (*passiflora*) is 2 inches long and thick, a dark purple, with yellow pulp, many seeds, and a semi-acid flavour between a melon and a strawberry. Perhaps the best and sweetest jungle fruit is the Morra, as big as a nutmeg, brown and with a rough case like an eggshell, inside which a good-sized black stone lies embedded in pulp like the flesh of a grape.

It is an almost hopeless task to give on paper any idea of the extraordinary beauty and variety of the Flowers and Ferns in Ceylon. Of the latter there are 270 species, including one kind in which the spores grow upon the upper instead of the under side of the frond. As for flowers, the earth is in many places literally carpeted with them, to an extent that defies even mere enumeration in these pages.

Foremost in beauty is the exquisite Night-flowering Cereus (*C. grandiflorus*), which begins to open soon after sunset, and is fully blown by eleven o'clock: long before dawn the flowers are hanging down faded, never again to expand. But during those few short hours there is no flower of greater magnificence, with its calyx of 10 or 12 inches in breadth, like the rays of a bright star, and white petals. On a large plant many blooms will appear in one night: I have seen as many as ten open at the same time. There is one species (*C. flagelliformis*) with a pink flower that remains open for three or four days.

Then there are the Orchids, a marvellous clan, of which there are 150 separate species, many of quite entrancing and fantastic beauty, such as

Dendrobium album, *aureum*, *pallidum*, etc. They are as plentiful as poppies in a Surrey cornfield, and are often found growing amongst the grass, or fixed upon pieces of matting stuck to the coco palms. The wonderful *Spirito santo* of Panama, with its dove-like flower, has here its counterpart in *Diparis atropurpurea*. *D. tripetaloidea* is just like an owl's head, with its pink flower and yellow lip. *Satyrium Nepalense* resembles a child's doll. *Oberonia Scyllæ* has a tiny crimson blossom that looks like a bunch of red tongues thrust out of a mask like a Gorgon. *Dendrobium Maccarthiæ* and the King of the forest (*Anæctochilus setaceus*) are of surpassing beauty, the latter, called by the natives *wanna-raja* and common in marshy ground, especially so. The delicate white flower upon a pink stalk is less attractive than the exquisite black velvet leaf reticulated with veins of gold and of a pale lake hue underneath. The Tiger orchid is striped, in accordance with its name, so that one may fancy it to have been developed on Darwinian principles out of some primordial tiger, which was rewarded by a floral apotheosis for abstinence from carnivorous diet.

There are noble Arum lilies in multitudes, the

huge purple bells of Thunbergia, the brown-yellow funnels of Aristolochia, the gay trumpet-shaped Bignonia, tall red lobelias, grand balsams, large purple gentians, violets, harebells, lilies of the valley, foxgloves, and many another old favourite, most of the more familiar ones being found only in the higher districts.

Here too is the singular Pitcher plant (*Nepenthes distillatoria*) or "monkey-jug," full of liquid, and in which under the cavity of the lid may often be found a number of too-curious captured flies. The liquid on analysis has been found to contain traces of vegetable matter together with minute crystals of superoxalate of potash. The plant shows an example of the provident economy of nature in the way in which the seeds are protected, each being furnished with a long loose integument, which acts both as a buoy to float the seed upon the water, and as an anchor to moor it in the mud until it strikes root.[1]

Vast numbers of exotics, such as the rose, geranium, sweet-pea, rose-periwinkle, sunflower, agave, aloe (a corruption of the Arabic *al 'ud*, meaning "the wood"), prickly pear, and among

[1] Note W.

vegetables the potato, cabbage, tomato, radish, etc., also form a part of the flora of Ceylon. In this beautiful "Eden of all plenteousness" there are no less than 2832 species of indigenous trees, plants, and flowers, a number twice as great as the total flora of the British Isles, and forming one-thirtieth part of the flora of the whole world.

> *No want was there of human sustenance,*
> *Soft fruitage, mighty nuts, and nourishing roots;*
> *The slender coco's drooping crown of plumes,*
> *The lightning flash of insect and of bird,*
> *The lustre of the long convolvuluses*
> *That coil'd around the stately stems, and ran*
> *Ev'n to the limit of the land, the glows*
> *And glories of the broad belt of the world,*
> *The moving whisper of huge trees that branch'd*
> *And blossom'd in the zenith.*

CHAPTER IX

GEMS, ETC.

In all ages of which we have any record Ceylon has been renowned for those gems which are said by the Mohammedans to be the tears of Adam after his expulsion from Eden. While making allowance for exaggerations, there is no doubt that in former times many fine stones have been found, of a size and brilliancy unsurpassed by those of any country in the world.[1] At the present day there are abundant specimens still to be seen, as the newly-arrived stranger at Colombo will quickly discover, possibly to his chagrin, inasmuch as many of those pressed upon his admiration are almost worthless, and in not a few cases mere fraudulent imitations. A friend of mine was shown a fine-looking sapphire for which the modest sum of £200 sterling was asked. Having

[1] Note X.

been warned of the extortionate demands made by the dealers, he offered the reduced sum of £4, which was promptly accepted. No sooner had the vendor disappeared over the ship's side than his victim ascertained that the gem was a bit of glass.

Most of the precious stones are found in the Moonstone, Elk, Totapella, and Horton plains, where there are many remains of deep pits dug by the searchers in old times. The surface soil is light and peaty, and overlies a stony stratum mixed with quartz gravel, evidently once subjected to the action of running water, and resting upon a stiff white clay. If it is desired to sink a new pit, the upper gravel is pierced near the edge of the bed of a stream in the summer time when the water is low. A hard crust (*cadua*) looking like sunburnt brick is met with, at the depth of some 20 feet, in the residuum of which, when broken up and washed free from sand in conical baskets, the gems are found.

All the Sapphire and Ruby species are classed under the generic name of Corundum, so called because these stones are composed of the same earth (*alumina*) as the corundum or *kurun* of India. Of the oriental ruby proper, called by the natives *ratha*, there are seven varieties, known among the Arab dealers by names signifying striped, hyacinth, bright red, brass coloured, red-wine coloured (amethyst), flesh coloured, and asafœtida coloured. The finest, varying from carmine to rose-red, are found at Rakwana and Ratnapoora (city of rubies), which has always been the capital of the gem district. Marco Polo mentions a ruby in the treasury of one of the kings, which was "a span in length, without a flaw and brilliant beyond words." Other writers have spoken of this same gem. In the sixth century a traveller said it was "as big as a great pine-cone, and when it is seen from a distance flashing, it is a glorious and incomparable spectacle." An English traveller 500 years ago tells us that "the king when going to be crowned takes the ruby in his hand, and goes round the city on horseback, and thenceforth all recognise and obey him as their king." The Arabs say that rubies purify the blood, quench thirst, dispel melancholy, avert danger, and ensure honour; and that a true gem when put in the fire becomes invisible, in water glows with heat, and in the dark shines like a hot coal. Pink rubies (*patmaraga*), light stones with a strong dash of pink, are rare, and if perfect command a high price.

Sapphires, native *nila*, vary in colour from a cornflower to a violet, and are sometimes found of large size; not many years ago one was sold for £4000. They are in five varieties—peacock-blue, azure, indigo, gray, and greenish. A white or water sapphire (*puspa raga*), known in Europe as the topaz, is not uncommon, and seems to differ from the true sapphire only in colour.[1]

I cannot give a scientific discrimination of the whole of the Ceylon gems. As a matter of fact, even among the natives themselves there is hopeless confusion in the matter of nomenclature. Nor did the ancients sufficiently distinguish between them. According to Theophrastus the sapphire was identical with *lapis lazuli*, which is now known to be a mineral. It is found in varying shapes, the best being like a hen's egg covered with a thin white stony coat, which when pounded requires neither washing nor polishing. The Arabs test a lapis lazuli by rubbing it upon a dry stone, when if false it becomes dark; they then put it in the mouth and afterwards in the

[1] Note Y.

fire, the true stone remaining undiscoloured. Lapis lazuli means "azure stone," lazuli standing for the Arabic *Lajward* (a place mentioned by Marco Polo as being famous for its mines), of which "azure" is a corruption.

Cat's-eyes (*vyrody*) are found both of the chatoyant pseudo-quartz and the true varieties. It is difficult for the tyro to distinguish between them, but when put side by side they cannot be mistaken: the true stone is yellow, brown, or green, iridescent and carrying a brilliant polish; the quartz, yellow or grayish-green, with a dull ray. The true cat's-eye, which is always found with sapphires, is really a rare variety of chrysoberyl, yielding in hardness only to the diamond and sapphire, and being venerated by the natives as a charm against witchcraft, is very unwillingly parted with. It is indeed a beautiful stone, remarkable for its soft deep colour and mysterious gleaming streak, which shifts from side to side with every movement.

Fine violet Amethysts are found, as well as Chrysolites of a yellow-green colour.

Garnet is abundant in the gneiss at Adam's Peak and Trincomalee. A rich claret-coloured sort called Almandine fetches a high price; in reality it is nothing but a carbuncle cut in a particular way. In the fourteenth century an emperor of China had a Ceylon carbuncle fitted as a ball in his cap, an ounce in weight and costing 100,000 strings of cash. Whenever a grand levée was held at night "the red lustre filled the palace, and hence it was designated the Red Palace Illuminator."

Ceylon is, I believe, the only country in which is found the variety of garnet called Jacinth, hyacinth, cinnamon stone, or essonite. It is orange-red in colour, and is found in considerable quantities and of a large size in the rocky mountainous strata. Moonstone or Selenite (Greek *aphroselene*, Latin *lunaris*) is (in the words of an old writer) "a kind of gem which doth contain the image of the moon, and doth represent it increasing and decreasing according to the increase and decrease of the moon in its monthly changes." It is a variety of pearly *adularia*, presenting chatoyant rays when simply polished. For many centuries the rest of the world has been supplied with moonstones from Ceylon, where they are now very cheap and possess little market value. I close this short list with the brittle Tourmaline, first brought to Europe by the Dutch, and of which the only variety found here is of a greeny-yellow hue.

Among metals and minerals Gold, although frequently found, has never been worked in sufficient quantities to make it payable. There is reason to believe that it is deficient neither in quantity nor quality. Nickel and Cobalt are sent to China in considerable quantities for the porcelain factories. Supplies of Plumbago are apparently inexhaustible, there being not less than 753 mines at work, yielding 30,000 tons a year, valued at 3,000,000 rupees. Iron ore is found pretty well all over the island, and in many places crops out at the surface of excellent quality. It is easily smelted, and produces from 50 to 75 per cent. Ceylon shares with the Ural mountains the distinction of being the only place whence is obtained the rare Tellurium, worth £20 a pound. Manganese and Nitre are abundant, as is a disintegrated felspar known as Kaolin, found near Galle and exported to China.

Lastly, large quantities of Salt are obtained

from some large lakes in the south near a small sea-coast town called Hambantotte. The water of these lakes is simply powerful brine. The yield is taken in August at the height of the dry season, by a very clumsy method. The natives go into the water after it, the result being painful excoriations of feet and legs. Salt is a government monopoly at three shillings a bushel.

CHAPTER X

PEARLS

PEARLS have formed for many centuries an important item in the natural products of Ceylon. The fishery is unfortunately at the present time nothing compared to what it was, its decadence being due in no small degree to the utterly reckless and wasteful manner in which it was carried on in the early part of the present century. It was under the government of Sir W. Horton (1831-37) that, in order to replenish the treasury, the goose that laid the golden eggs was grievously injured, an operation from which it has never entirely recovered.

In former days the kings of Ceylon were wont to style themselves "Lords of the pearl fishery." So far as history goes, the year B.C. 306 is the date of the earliest native records of a fishing, at which time the banks appear to have received much damage from an extraordinary inundation of the sea. From this fact it is assumed that the site of the fishing grounds was not where it is now, about 150 miles from Colombo, but farther to the north, between the island and the mainland, in the Gulf of Manaar,[1] at or near Adam's Bridge, which stretches from Manaar to Ramasserum Island.

The Bridge is described in the government chart as a bank of sand lying upon a bed of soft sandstone rock, with many scours or shallow channels intersecting it, through some of which small boats can pass in fine weather. Baldæus says that in the seventeenth century Teuver, the governor of the country, sold to the Portuguese a passage through the straits, "which he commands by either laying stones or removing them from the entrance."

Pliny (ix. 54) informs us that "the Indians seek for pearls in Taprobane, which is the most productive of them:" a statement confirmed by Ælian, who, moreover, gives the palm to them over

[1] *Manaar* is Tamul for a sandy river. In the *Ramayana* is recorded how Rama, with his army of angels in the form of monkeys, threw a bridge across the sea between Lanka (Ceylon) and the mainland, along which they passed and laid siege to the fortress of the giant Ravanna, whom they slew, and delivered the earth from the enormities of his tyranny. Rama was the most illustrious of the Suryavansas, or solar line of Indian kings, and was the son of Dhusarutha, king of Oudh.

those found in the Persian Gulf, a distinction which in more recent times they appear to have forfeited. Ralph Fitch, who visited Ceylon at the end of the sixteenth century, records that "the best pearls come from the Iland of Baharim in the Persian sea, the woorser from the Piscaria, neere the Isle of Ceylon." Many centuries before Christ Chinese writers recorded the size and excellence of the island pearls.

It is well known that pearls of some value are occasionally found in other than the true pearl oyster. Twenty centuries ago, according to Suetonius, the Romans used to get them from Britain. "It is a fact," says the inexhaustible Pliny (ix. 35), "that in Britannia pearls are found, though small and of a bad colour; for the deified Julius Cæsar wished it to be plainly understood that the breastplate which he presented to Venus Genetrix was made of British pearls." According to Tacitus, in his *Life of Agricola*, they were "subfusca ac liventia," not very bright but pale. Origen and the Venerable Bede both speak of them. Seed pearls are, or used to be not long ago, on sale at Conway in large numbers, at a price varying from five to ten shillings an ounce. Many of these both in early and later times were not the product of the pearl mussel (*Unio margaritifera*), but of an inferior one (*Mytilus edulis*). The classical authority upon the subject of British pearls is a paper by Sir R. Redding, printed in the *Philosophical Transactions* for 1693. The author gives high praise to the pearls of Ireland, where he tells us that the poor people used to fish for them in the warm weeks just before harvest, and call them *cregin diliuw* or deluge shells: they took them out with their toes or with wooden tongs, or by "thrusting a stick into the shells as they lay with the white foot protruded like a tongue out of the mouth." One in a hundred might contain a gem, of which the same proportion might be tolerably clear. He adds that "some gentlemen of the country made a good advantage thereof, and I myself saw one pearl bought for fifty shillings that weighed thirty-six carats and was valued at £40. A miller took out a pearl which he sold for ninety shillings to a man who sold it for £10, who sold it to Lady Glenealy for £30, who refused an offer of £80 from the Duchess of Ormonde." On the authority of Pennant we learn that Sir Richard Wynne of

Gwydir, chamberlain to Catharine, Queen of Charles II., "presented her Majesty with a pearl from Conway, which is to this day honoured with a place in the royal crown." Scottish pearls also were, as they are still, held in some repute. In the *Magazine of Natural History* for June 1830 one is mentioned as measuring half an inch in diameter, and a Captain Brown at the end of the last century records that gems were frequently found in the Teith and the Tay worth one or two pounds each.

The conchiferous bivalve mollusc (*Maleagrina margaritifera*), known in English as the Pearl Oyster, and in Singhalese as *mootoo*, bears a close resemblance both outside and in to the edible oyster of Europe; but its unequal valves, one cupped, the other flat, as well as its general size and shape, will always make it known as the pearl oyster, notwithstanding its classification by Linnæus as a mussel. Unlike the edible fish, pearl oysters have a broad hinge to the shells, and a fibrous *byssus* or beard of a dark sea-green colour, by means of which they adhere to each other in clusters.

In the spring months the spawn or spat of the fish floats in large quantities upon the top of the sea, and after a while gradually sinks, through the increase of weight caused by the deposition of earthy and other matter. It then falls and settles upon the bottom in heaps of brood oysters, the proportion that in due time reaches maturity depending greatly upon the depth of water and the character of the ground. Large numbers fall a prey before the shell is hardened to other fish, chiefly a kind called by the natives *pottooberre*, an oval thick-skinned fish a foot long, from one of which as many as ten pearls have been taken. Some of the young oysters that fall upon a clear sandy bed adhere to one another, others cling by their beards with great tenacity to rocks and large shells. It is asserted by Kelaart and other observers that not only can the pearl oyster at its own will detach itself, but that it is not more remarkable for its tenacity of life than for its locomotive powers.

And now, what about the pearl itself? The common oriental belief is that the gems are

> *Rain from the sky*
> *Which turns into pearls as it falls in the sea.*

A substance so unlike the composition of the shell in which it is found naturally gave rise to many speculations as to its origin, before science had determined its real nature. Pliny tells us that the oyster produces the pearl by feeding upon heavenly dew. Boethius, writing about British pearls, says that "these mussels early in the morning open their mouths a little above the water, and most greedily swallow the dew of heaven; and after the measure and quantity of the dew which they swallow, they conceive and breed the pearl. These mussels," he adds, "are so exceedingly quick of touch and hearing, that however faint the noise that may be made on the bank beside them, they sink at once to the bottom, knowing well in what estimation the fruit of their womb is to all people."

Alas! the sledge hammer of science has in this, as in many other directions, smashed up poesy and romance, converting not only the diamond into vulgar charcoal, but the pearl into concentric layers of membrane and carbonate of lime. It has been proved that the gem pearl is simply a protection made by the mollusc to secure itself against the presence of grains of sand and other irritants. Linnæus showed that by perforating a live pearl oyster and introducing a grain, a nucleus is formed for the development of the gem. The grain falls upon the mantle-lobes, and sets up an irritant action resulting in the formation of a nacreous substance over and around the intruding particle, which in time becomes a pearl. There are various minute boring *Annelidæ* which perforate the oyster shell, inducing for the repair of the injury an abnormal secretion of nacre from the "mantle" under the spot attacked, by which means nuclei are formed which by constant enlargement become pearl gems. Other naturalists have thought that the gem is merely a product of disease, caused by the overcharge of the glands of the iridescent nacreous fluid; but the theory of Linnæus is now more widely accepted.

The substance known as mother-of-pearl is a shining excretion or nacre deposited upon the inner surfaces in successive layers, and found in a larger shell than the gem, being often 12 inches across.

The pearl oyster takes five years in reaching maturity, after which the beard begins to break, owing to the increasing weight of the shells, and the fish leaves the substance to which it has been so long fastened. Between the age of five and seven years, which is considered to be the extreme limit, the pearls are at their best.

The method of fishing them is now substantially what it has always been. "The pearl fishers," says Marco Polo, "take their vessels great and small, and proceed into this gulf [between the island of Seilan and the mainland], where they stop from the beginning of April till the middle of May [now a month earlier]. They go first to a place called Bettelar [now Patlam], and then go 60 miles into the gulf. Here they cast anchor and shift from their large vessels into small boats. . . . When the men have got into the small boats they jump into the water and dive to the bottom, which may be at a depth of from 4 to 12 fathoms, and there they remain as long as they are able. And there they find shells that contain the pearls, and these they put into a net bag tied round the waist, and mount up to the surface with them, and then dive anew: when they can't hold their breath any longer they come up again, and after a little down they go once more, and so they go on all day."

The present fishing grounds are on the west coast of the island, opposite to a long desolate stretch of barren sand, near the little Cutcherry stream, where at the edge of some palms and a straggling thorny jungle stands Kondachi, a mere ghost of a hamlet, with the larger village of Aripo 4 miles away. Kondachi proper stands 2 miles farther up, at the head of a small bay, on the northern side of which is Silawatorre, the real landing-place of the boats with their cargoes. Here are to be seen, and smelt, gigantic mounds of oyster shells, many of whose original contents are gleaming now upon the fair necks of dames and damsels under a northern sky, but which here form a stinking mass of corruption, stretching along the shore for several miles, the accumulation of centuries.

Almost deserted for ten months in the year save by countless crabs and turtles, the month of February no sooner comes round than the whole scene is changed as if by magic, supposing, that is to say, that a fishing has been proclaimed. This event is contingent upon the report of the government inspector, who four or five months before makes a careful examination of the beds, and reports upon the probable results. If his report is favourable, notice is given in the following form, which I copy from a Colombo newspaper of some years back :—

> Government Advertisement. Pearl Fishery. Notice is hereby given that a Pearl Fishery will take place at Aripo, in the island of Ceylon, on or about the first day of March next, and that the Banks to be fished are as follows [here follow the names]. It is therefore recommended to such Boat Owners and Divers as may wish to be employed at the said Fishery that they should be at Aripo on or before the twentieth day of February next. The number of Boats to be employed will be One Hundred for seventeen days. The Fishery will be conducted on account of Government, and the oysters put up to Sale in such lots as may be deemed expedient.

Of the boats or *dhonies* thus applied for the best are chosen either by selection or by lots drawn among the *tindals* or masters, each successful applicant paying thirty shillings for a license to fish. Sometimes the privilege of fishing a certain bed, with a fixed number of boats and for a certain time, is put up at auction and sold to the highest bidder; sometimes the fishing is made and the proceeds are sold direct by Government; in either case the Government takes three-fourths of the whole catch, the boats' crew getting a quarter. In Marco Polo's time the fishermen used to give one-tenth to the king.

The scene at Aripo in the sixteenth century

was much the same during a fishery as it is now. Here is a description of it from the pen of Cæsar Fredericke in 1563: "Right agaynst that place where greatest store Oisters bee, there they make or plant a village with houses and a Bazaro, all of stone, which standeth as long as the fishing time lasteth, and it is furnished with all things necessarie. The Fishermen are all Christians of the countrey, and who so will may goe to fishing, paying a certaine dutie to the king of Portugall, and to the Churches of the Friers of Saint Paule, which are in that coast." As to the results he adds: "At evening they come to the village, and then every companie maketh their mountaine or heape of oysters one distant from another, in such wise that you shall see a great long rowe of mountaines or heapes, and they are not touched untill such time as the fishing bee ended, and at the ende of the fishing every companie setteth round about their heape and fall to opening of them, which they may easilie doe because they bee dead, drie and brittle."

There is little difference now. An impromptu fair or bazaar springs up along the shore, of huts and sheds made of palm leaves, mats, cotton-cloth, straw, and boards. The crustaceans have all betaken themselves to quieter regions, and in their stead the whole place is alive with a motley rabble of snake-charmers, jugglers, fishermen, speculators, dancing-girls, vagabonds, and fakirs, in all or no costumes, among them some of the most disgusting objects to be seen anywhere on earth; while yonder the sapphire sea is stirred from its silence by hundreds of canoes and catamarans laden to the water with food and necessaries for the multitude.

Evening comes, and by ten or eleven o'clock the fishing fleet is ready to start. The dhonies, each with a crew of fourteen men besides the divers (*kooly karer*), are 30 or 40 feet long, 10 feet in beam, from 8 to 10 tons burden, and made with raking stem and stern-post: they have a mast and lugsail, and are quite unmanageable in a rough sea. The first thing to be done is for the divers, who are chiefly Malabars, Tamuls, and Moormen, to secure themselves against the ravages of the tiger of the deep. This they effect to their own satisfaction by means of charms dispensed by men who are known by the Tamuls as *pillal-kadtar*, by the Singhalese as *kadal-katti*, others Abraim, or shark-binders. Marco Polo tells us that these in his time received a fee of one-twentieth of the catch, and he adds that "the charm lasteth but one day, as at night they dissolve the charm, so that the fish can work mischief at their will." At the diamond mines of the northern Circars Brahmans are employed in a similar office as propitiators of the tutelary genii. These charmers have no real right nowadays to the name of Abraim or Brahmans, whatever they may have been in former times. They all belong to one family, which is supposed to hold the monopoly of the power. The chief operator is now paid by Government the sum of ninepence a day, in addition to which he gets ten oysters per diem from each dhony. Should there be any Christian divers, as sometimes happens among the Malabars, they are presented by a Roman Catholic priest with rosaries and amulets made of palm leaves. Not many years ago the principal shark-binder himself was a Christian, a fact which did not apparently, in the native mind, affect the validity of his charms.

As to the efficacy of these mystical precautions, I will not venture an opinion, but the fact remains that, although the divers are possessed by such terror of sharks that if but one is seen near the boats the fishing is at once suspended for the rest of the day, there is not a single instance on record of any injury done. The risk is far less than might be supposed. There is too much noise and splashing, and the dark-skinned bodies do not attract the sharks—a fact so well understood that in the Persian Gulf the divers often darken their lighter skins. Far more to be feared is the terrible saw-fish, which occasionally runs amuck through the divers, carrying off an arm or a leg in his career.

Arrived at the fishing ground, which lies from 6 to 10 miles out at sea (the largest off Aripo being 10 miles long by 2 wide), a flag is run up on the guard-ship and the divers prepare for action. Unlike the Persians, who fill their ears with cotton steeped in oil and compress the nose with a bit of tortoise-shell, the diver at Aripo simply puts his foot into a sinking-stone, takes a deep breath, squeezes his nostrils with the left hand, and slips feet foremost over the side. The sinking-stone is conical or pear-shaped, weighing from 25 to 30 pounds, and hung at the end of a double coir rope: the net, commonly called a basket, is made of coir yarn 18 inches wide and the same deep, and is hung by a single cord only, so that when under water the diver may not mistake between the two. The bight of the double one is passed over a stick projecting from the boat, to enable the diver to adjust exactly the weight of the stone. He puts his right foot on the stone, gets the double end between his toes, and places his left foot in the rim of the net hoop, which he at the same moment presses firmly between his knees. Then he takes his dive, and immediately on reaching the bottom, which is never more than 10 fathoms deep, he slips his foot from the stone and sets to work on all fours to fill his net with shells as fast as he can. After 60 or 70 seconds he jerks the rope and is swiftly drawn up at the end of the net. When near the surface he lets go, puts his arms close to his side with his hands upon his thighs, and comes bounding up head and shoulders above the water. No sooner is the net emptied than he is ready to go down again, and will repeat the performance 40 or 50 times between sunrise and noon, during which time he will bring up perhaps 2000 or 3000 shells, thus earning about £4 sterling a week. The work is no doubt trying, but perhaps more so in appearance than reality. Blood frequently oozes from mouth, ears, and nose, but is regarded as a useful means of relieving the extreme pressure upon the head.

The most favourable weather for fishing is when soon after sunrise the land wind dies away and is followed at noon by a sea breeze. If the north-east wind continues to blow the boats do not go out, to which cause of delay are sometimes added the superstitious notions of the divers with regard to certain lucky and unlucky days, in which matter their prejudices are always considered.

At noon the flag is hauled down, work ceases, and the boats make for land either before a westerly breeze or with their long oars out. They are at once unladen and a general sale is held. The shells fetch all prices from 15 shillings to £6 or £8 a thousand, according to the season and the number caught. A couple can be bought as a speculation for three halfpence. A poor man once bought three for that sum, and found the largest pearl of the season. Of course the chances are varied and tempting: one boat may have 30,000 on board, another not half; as many as 2,000,000 have been landed by one dhony as the result of a week's work. In 1814 no less than 76,000,000 shells were offered for sale in one week; but in 1859 the number did not average more than 10,000,000. The pale pink pearls, although very beautiful, do not command the highest prices, any more than do of necessity the largest. The really costly ones are the round, bright, translucent, silvery-white gems, smooth and stainless, that are found growing upon the actual flesh of the oyster; those adhering to the shell, useful for rings, brooches, etc., have always one side imperfect.

The sale over, the buyers either open the shells at once, bury them in the sand, or store them in hollow pits called *cottoos*, open repositories paved with brick and covered with chunam. This is done in order to hasten the decomposition of the fish, the result being a mass of semi-corruption, that taints the air for miles. Strange to say, no bad results seem to follow, owing possibly to the well-known fact that in all tropical lands vegetable decomposition is far more deleterious than animal.

When ready the shells are thrown into *ballams*, a kind of dug-out canoe 20 or 30 feet long, 3 wide, and 2 deep: salt water is poured on them and they are carefully looked over. Those with pearls are set apart, those with none are thrown in heaps upon the sand. The washing process is then repeated again and again until all the mud and sand are cleared away, and the gems deposited in the water; women and children then strain the water in search of seed pearls, about the size of small shot; after which all are sorted, weighed, and valued, by being screened through a succession of brass colanders each in succession with smaller holes, the topmost and smallest one having the largest. Throughout the whole proceedings a careful watch is kept by Government officers, whose vigilance is sometimes eluded by the natives, who now and then swallow the gems or conceal them in their hair.

As for the value of the fishery it varies very much, and has been carried on from time to time under different conditions. When the Portuguese were masters they had to buy the right of fishing from the ruler of Madura. Their successors, the Dutch, had constant trouble over the fisheries, but managed to make out of them about a quarter of a million sterling. At the beginning of the present century the English Government agreed to give the prince of Madura one-tenth of the proceeds, an arrangement which brought nearly £3000 a year to his treasury, and lasted until 1839. For some years the fishery was worth to England large sums annually, never falling below £40,000; a great drop, however, from 1797, when it had realised £150,000. From 1837 to 1857 the pearls were never taken, except by poachers, to check whose ravages a guard was maintained at an annual expense of £850.

At Trincomalee on the east coast, in the Bay of Tamblecam, there is another fishing ground, where small pearls are found in a thin transparent oyster (*Placuna placenta*), of which the shells are exported to China, where they are used as window glass.

The following list of the value of the pearl fishery in rupees is taken, in round numbers, from the Colonial Office list:—

Year.	Rupees.
1860	375,000
1874	101,500
1879	84,500

Year.	Rupees.
1880	200,000
1881	600,000
1884	33,600
1887	401,000
1888	800,000
1889	500,000
1890 (approx.)	300,000

The true guarantee of the future continued prosperity of Ceylon is not to be found in the fluctuating harvest of the sea. It lies rather in her magnificent geographical position, her ready command of cheap labour, her superb climate, and the amazing fecundity with which Nature, out of a lean rather than a fat soil, pours forth her fruits in answer to human toil. As an emporium of commerce, a coaling station, and a half-way house for the far East, China, and Australia, the place of Ceylon on the map is unrivalled. To the traveller, apart from the cyclopean antiquities which will no doubt before long be made accessible to the madding crowd by a railway—conductors, coupons, and all the rest of it—there are abounding attractions in this beautiful island, be he artist or *ennuyé*, sportsman, naturalist, or scribe. The way there is in these days as easy as rolling off a log: it is only the way back that is hard; hard because, as the low palm-fringed shores sink beneath the horizon, and the Peak of Adam cloaks itself afar in a mantle of majestic mystery, you feel and know that yonder flashing point of light in your wake keeps watch by the gateway of an Eden where you fain would have lingered, and marks the portal of a summer isle wherein the brain-fogged workman may stand apart from the stress and strain of life, and the lotus-eater take his fill.

L'Envoi

WHERE whispering palms their tender love-tales tell
    With sun-flecked shadows to the pearl-gemmed shore,
    Hushed and afar Life's billows seem to roar,
Low as the magic murmur of the shell.

From thee, fair Orient Queen, I sadly part,
    Dear isle of peace, 'mid purple seas firm set,
    Thy face and form how can I e'er forget?
My steps may wander, but thou hast my heart.

NOTES

NOTE A, page 5

Sir Emerson Tennent has pointed out that although we cannot apply the term "hybernation" to the action of those physical causes which accompany their partial or total torpidity, there are nevertheless corresponding phenomena to be observed in many of the lower animals during the hot season in tropical lands. In the fierce heat of March and April myriads of insects, no longer able to obtain their accustomed food, disappear beneath the surface of the soil, or make to themselves hiding-places under fragments of wood; water-beetles strive to attain *nirvana* by burying themselves head over ears in the hard baked mud of the water-holes; slugs and snails retire into crevices among the stones or the hollow roots of trees. You may go a day's march and never see a *papilio*, and scarcely a bird; even the few that flit past you are dejected in appearance, and less sprightly on the wing; while the elephant, the wild buffalo, and the crocodile, impelled by a maddening craving for water, wander restlessly through the nearer jungles, or venture to moisten their parched throats at the village wells.

NOTE B, page 13

On his sixth voyage Sinbad was shipwrecked on the coast of Ceylon, at the foot of a mountain whose stones were crystals and rubies. He constructed a raft upon which he floated along an underground stream for some days in darkness. On waking from sleep he found himself at length in a plain surrounded by "negroes," who had made his raft fast to the bank. "Brother," said one to him in Arabic, "be not surprised to see us; we are inhabitants of this country, and came hither to water our fields, by digging little canals from this river which comes out of the neighbouring mountain." They then took him to the capital in the middle of the island, and presented him to their king. This subterranean exploit of Sinbad finds an illustration in the existing Singhalese belief that a stream actually exists which shows its connection with a marine source by a slight rise and fall during the twelve hours. It is known as the Well of Potoor.

Sinbad describes the island as being eighty parasangs in length and width, "situated just under the equatorial line, so that the days and nights are always of twelve hours each." Of the royal state he says: "When the king appears in public, he has a throne fixed on the back of an elephant, and marches betwixt two ranks of his ministers, favourites, and other people of his court; before him, upon the same elephant, an officer carries a golden lance in his hand; and behind the throne there is another, who stands upright with a column of gold, on the top side of which is an emerald half a foot long and an inch thick; before him marches a guard of 1000 men, clad in cloth of gold and silk, and mounted on elephants richly caparisoned. And one went before him crying, 'Behold the monarch greater than Solomon, and the powerful Maha-râja!' And the officer behind cries in his turn, 'This monarch, so great and so powerful, must die, must die, must die.'"

On his seventh voyage Sinbad again visited Ceylon, and delivered a costly present to the king from Haroun al Raschid.

It was on his return from this voyage that he was seized by corsairs and landed on another island, where he saw the place to which all the elephants came for burial when they were conscious of approaching death.

NOTE C, page 44

Marignolli says: "Cain was a vagabond who wandered about the earth, and was thought to have built Cotta, in Seyllen. The Veddahs were descended from him; their faces were hideous and frightful, and their wives equally ugly. They were wanderers who could never stay two days in one place."

NOTE D, page 45

On the doctrines of Buddha see T. W. Rhys Davids's *Buddhism*. A popular account of them is given in Chambers's *Information for the People*, vol. ii. p. 427. It is enough to say here that, strictly speaking, Buddhism knows nothing either of worship, sacraments, or liturgy. The cult consists of meditation, preaching, reading the *Sutras* (forming the second division of the *Pitakattayan*, see p. 23 note), and offerings. The images of Buddha (which are an innovation) are regarded less as idols, in our sense of the word, than as sacred memorials of one who has ceased to exist in form, and who is before his votaries as an ideal model of what all may become by following his example.

NOTE E, page 55

"In the chewing of the areca nut, with its accompaniments of lime and betel, the native of Ceylon is unconsciously applying a specific corrective to the defective qualities of his daily food. Never eating flesh meat by any chance, seldom or never using milk, butter, poultry, or eggs, and tasting fish but occasionally (more rarely in the interior of the island), the non-azotised elements abound in every article he consumes, with the exception of the breadfruit, the jak, and some varieties of beans. In their indolent and feeble stomach these are liable to degenerate into flatulent and acrid products; but, apparently by instinct, the whole population have adopted a simple prophylactic. No medical prescription could be more judiciously compounded to effect the desired object than this practical combination of the antacid, the tonic, and the carminative" (Tennent).

NOTE F, page 69

Dr. Wagner and Dr. Supan, the editors of the *Bevölkerung der Erde* (Gotha, 1891), set down the total population of the globe at the present time as 1,479,000,000, of which 825,000,000 belong to Asia, and rather less than half that number to Europe.

NOTE G, page 83

The age of the famous tree in the island of Teneriffe, at the date of its final destruction by a storm in 1867, estimated by some at 6000 years, was purely traditionary. A young tree is now flourishing in the exact spot where its parent stood for so many centuries. The *Dracæna draco*, which in appearance resembles rather a giant plant than a tree, is far surpassed in size and picturesqueness by the chestnut of Etna, the *castagno di cento cavalli* in East Sicily, which gets its name from a company of knights who, with one of the queens of Aragon, found shelter under its branches. Its reputed age is 1000 years. Humboldt saw a cypress (*Taxodium distichum*) at Chapultepec whose age he estimated at 6000 years.

It is perhaps not superfluous to remind my readers that no satisfactory evidence of the age of a tree is afforded either by its girth or by the number of its concentric rings. Such an idea once held by the most eminent botanists is now exploded. Mons. D. Charnay, the well-known French savant, visited the ruins of Palenque in Central America in 1859, and for photographic purposes cut down all the trees that in the course of centuries had taken root among the masses of masonry. On revisiting the place in 1881 he found that other trees had grown up, one of which had attained in 22 years a diameter of 2 feet and contained 230 concentric circles. We cannot therefore estimate the age of trees, at least in tropical lands, by any such rough-and-ready mode of calculation.

NOTE H, page 93

The spire and bell-shaped dome is the distinguishing feature of all dagobas, although in contour and details of workmanship there is endless diversity. In not a few instances the spire springs from a square base surmounting a dome which stands on a quadrangular platform flanked by a circular fosse, giving a fantastic alternation of circle, quadrate, and hemisphere. The material of which the dagoba is made is for the most part bricks and mortar coated with chunam, coco-nut water, and the glutinous juice of the ebony fruit (*Diospyros ebenus*). In the centre of the structure is a small chamber or receptacle for the preservation of the sacred relics, which when once deposited are never disturbed.

NOTE I, page 94

Among the most curious relics seen here and there among these marvellous ruins desolated by twice two thousand monsoons, are small square blocks of stone each with a number of square hollows pierced in it varying in number from ten to twenty. I was at a loss to understand their purpose or significance until it was explained to me that they were used by the priests for the following not very intelligible ends. After pouring into each of the hollows certain ingredient charms, consisting of oil, spices, etc., the priest took his stand in front of the stone and fixed his eyes intently upon it in a kind of spiritual ecstasy. Thus he would remain for a long time lost to all outward things, until a divine recognition of his faith and patience was vouchsafed in the form of a tiny ray of light kindled in the centre of the stone. As he gazed with deepening awe and rapt intensity there gradually opened up before him a vision of the depths of the infernal regions, succeeded as he raised his eyes to heaven by a revelation of the "Elysian fields" and the abodes of the demigods; until, finally, as the apocalyptic vision landed him on the highest pinnacle of sacerdotal exaltation, his soul was bathed in the beatific glories of the *nirvana*, highest state of all.

For a modern digest of the depressing doctrine of *nirvana* see Arnold's *Light of Asia*, book viii. The idea at the root of it is to be blown out at death like a candle. To a Western mind such a theory appears very remorseless, for men in the West are fuller of life and hope than Orientals, who are so imbued with the uselessness of fighting against fate that they turn with delight to the Buddha, who tells them that happiness can only be reached by destroying the capacity for emotion. Nor in England is the number decreasing of those who discern in the teaching of the Buddhistic books much that they were already familiar with in the splendid fragments of Cædmon.

NOTE J, page 110

The mention of Sinbad reminds me that his story of the loadstone mountain which drew out the iron bolts of passing ships is alluded to by several Arabian writers, and can be traced back to very early Chinese authors. At the present day a Singhalese makes his boat with bolts of wood instead of iron nails, in exact accordance with the precept of Palladius that "vessels sailing for Ceylon should be fastened with wooden and not iron bolts."

NOTE K, page 119

In the small but exquisite tomb mosque of Kaitbey at Cairo there are two blocks of rose granite bearing the impress of Mohammed's feet, who is said to rest there for a few moments each Thursday at sunset. They are veiled by small curtains with canopies, one of bronze, the other of wood.

NOTE L, page 134

The solemn benediction of the people by the priest is but one of many points of resemblance between Buddhistic and Catholic ritual. The Abbé Huc gives the following list: "La crosse, la mitre, la dalmatique, la chape ou pluvial, l'office à deux chœurs, la psalmodie, les exorcismes, l'encensoir soutenu par cinq chaines, les bénédictions données par les Lamas en étendant la main droite sur la tête des fidèles ; le chapelet, le célibat ecclesiastique, les processions, les litanies, l'eau bénite." To which may be added the tonsure, the confessional, the solemn commemoration of the departed, and the veneration of relics.

NOTE M, page 142

The duration of a proboscidian's life has long been a matter of conjecture. Professor Owen is of opinion that 100 years fairly represents its average age. One individual was known during the Portuguese and Dutch occupation to have worked for at least 140. It is at any rate possible that two or three generations of the elephant have witnessed the many violent changes which during the last four centuries have overthrown the native dynasties and brought the island under the British crown.

NOTE N, page 165

As many as 10,000 of these squid "pens" have been found inside one whale. The calamary (*Sepiola Atlantica*), a mollusc allied to the octopus of the *Teuthidæ* family, forms a favourite article of human food in the Ægean islands, and I have myself eaten it at the Cappello Nerò, in Venice, fried with lemons.

NOTE O, page 170

This species, in common with *B. pica* and *B. bicornis*, possesses a huge beak, of which one of the functions is vouched for by Mr. Edgar Layard in Ceylon, by Dr. Livingstone in Africa, and Mr. Wallace in Sumatra. When the hen bird has laid her egg and taken to the nest for the purpose of incubation, her mate carefully closes up the hole in the tree where the nest is, and leaves just a space large enough for him to pass his bill through with the necessary food.

NOTE P, page 175

The *Pratyasatka* tells us that "nothing can improve the crows," and that "in wrath for their tale-bearing—for had they not carried abroad the secrets of the councils of the gods?—Indra hurled them down through the hundred storeys of his heaven" (E. L. Arnold's *Bird Life*).

NOTE Q, page 183

Sea-snakes are held in great detestation by fishermen, because they frequently entangle themselves in the nets, and when hauled up are unwittingly handled with very unpleasant results. It is not generally known that their fangs contain poison of the most deadly nature. Some years ago a midshipman on the Indian station in H.M.S. *Wolf* was bitten by a sea-snake brought up in a dredging net, and from refusing to have the wound properly treated, died in great pain. The wounds are exceedingly small, and look at first no worse than a mosquito bite, but in a few hours partial suffocation, enlargement of the tongue, and rigidity of the muscles ensue, followed by death. The eyes of the *hydrophides* are so adapted for seeing under the water that when on land they become blind, and in their writhings sometimes bite their own bodies.

NOTE R, page 193

This fish is closely allied to the fossil fishes found, in conjunction with the pandanus, custard-apple, etc., in the clay of the Isle of Sheppey.

NOTE S, page 193

Bêche-de-mer is a mollusc, one of the *Holothurides*, called by the Chinese *tripang*, and in appearance like a great slug. Like other creatures of the same type, it lives by suction, and possesses the simplest possible anatomy. When disturbed, it imbibes and ejects through its three-cornered mouth a great quantity of water,—an operation which appears indeed to form its principal amusement at all times. There are several varieties, of which the gray is most valued, but the black and the spotted are the largest, reaching a length of 2 feet. Bêche-de-mer soup is often seen in the bill of fare at Australian hotels and restaurants, and is eaten to an enormous extent in China, where it is worth from £80 to £90 a ton.

NOTE T, page 195

Professor Grant of Edinburgh says: "My two living *tritonia*, contained in a large clear colourless glass cylinder, filled with pure salt water and placed on the central table of the Wernerian

Natural History Society of Edinburgh, around which many members were sitting, continued to clink audibly within the distance of 12 feet during the whole meeting. These small animals were individually not half the size of the last joint of my little finger. What effect the mellow sounds of millions of these covering the shallow bottom of a tranquil estuary, in the silence of night, might produce, I can scarcely conjecture."

NOTE U, page 241

Sometimes, however, Miss Flora sets her own music going. The world of vegetation in the tropics often pours forth strains under the influence of the winds, bringing to mind that music which Prospero commanded. The sailor, flung by the white surf upon the shores of Ceylon, might fancy himself in an enchanted island, as he listened to the sounds of melody in the air. Sir Emerson Tennent says of the vocal bamboo: "On drawing near to a clump of trees, above the branches of which waved a slender bamboo about 50 feet in length, musical tones issued from it caused by the breeze passing through perforations in the stem."

NOTE V, page 260

A stranger in the tropics often wonders at the delicious coolness of many of the fruits even in the hottest weather, and is at a loss to account for it. More than a century ago Dr. Blagden, the Secretary of the Royal Society, communicated to that learned body the results of certain personal experiments, in which he showed the power of the human frame to maintain a normal temperature of 96° Fahrenheit in a medium hot enough to cook a beefsteak. He explained it by the rapid transpiration and evaporation which takes place from the surface of the skin. Only when a drop of perspiration happened to fall before evaporating and scalded the part of the body which it touched, was any inconvenience felt by the experimentalist. The common phenomenon of the coldness of a healthy dog's nose illustrates the influence of evaporation in keeping the temperature of a part below that of the rest of the body, and indeed often lower than that of the surrounding atmosphere.

NOTE W, page 267

Insectivorous plants are of two kinds; those in which there is a true digestive process, and those in which there is nothing more than absorption of the liquid products. From their poor roots it would be impossible for them to obtain sufficient nitrogen unless they could entrap insects. The process of digestion is found at work in many different species of the vegetable kingdom, including the papaya or pawpaw, the leaves of which wrapped round tough meat make it tender in a few hours. The Boers of South Africa use *Roridula dentata*, one of the largest of the class, as a fly-catcher; when washed it can be used again and again.

NOTE X, page 269

Sinbad says: "Rubies and several sorts of minerals abound, and the rocks are for the most part composed of a metallic stone made use of to cut and polish other precious stones. There is also a pearl fishery in the mouth of its principal river, and in one of its valleys are found diamonds." In the letter sent by the king to Haroun al Raschid he describes himself as living "in a palace that shines with one hundred thousand rubies," and having in his treasury "twenty thousand crowns enriched with diamonds." Accompanying the missive was a present consisting of—1, a single ruby made into a cup, about ½ foot high, 1 inch thick, and filled with round pearls of half a drachm each; 2, the skin of a serpent with scales "as large as an ordinary piece of gold, and with the virtue of preserving from sickness those who lay upon it"; 3, 50,000 drachms of the best wood of aloes, with 30 grains of camphire "as big as pistachios"; 4, a female slave "of ravishing beauty, whose apparel was all covered over with jewels."

NOTE Y, page 272

In ancient times the Chinese used to distinguish the Ceylon varieties of topaz by names which signified the following colours: 1, wine; 2, young goslings; 3, deep amber like bees' wax; 4, the opening buds of the pine.

APPENDIX I

LIST OF PRINCIPAL KINGS, ETC.

Fourth visit of Buddha	B.C.	577
Wijayo I.		543
Panduwasa		504
Devenipiatissa (built many temples and tanks)		306
Tisso I. (built Thuparamaya)		280
Suratissa		247
Sena and Gutika (Malabar usurpers)		246
Asela		214
Elala (Tamul prince)		205
Dutu-Gaimono (built brazen palace)		164
Walagam-bahu (deposed by Malabars)		104
,, restored		90
Kuda-tissa (poisoned by his wife Anula)		50
Anula		47
Wijayo II.	A.D.	241
Singha-tissa I.		242
Mahasen (built Mineri tank)		275
Arrival of the Sacred Tooth from India		302
Mitta-sena (killed by Malabar invaders)		433
Anuradhapoora deserted for Pollonaruwa		729
Universal anarchy		1059
Prakrama-bahu I.		1153
Prakrama II.		1211
Wikrama III.		1371

Wijayo-bahu (carried to China) . . .	A.D. 1408
Island tributary to China . . .	1412-1461
Portuguese rule began	1505
Dutch rule began	1658
British rule began	1795
Wikrama (last native king, exiled) . . .	1815

APPENDIX II

A LIST OF WORKS ON CEYLON

Baker, Sir S. W. "Eight Years' Wanderings in Ceylon." Lond., 1874.

,, "Rifle and Hound in Ceylon." Lond., 1874.

Baldæus, P. "A true and exact Description of the Isle of Ceylon, etc., by P. Baldæus, minister of the word of God in Ceylon." Amsterdam, 1672.

Barrow, Sir G., Bart. "Ceylon Past and Present." London, 1857.

Bennett, J. W. "Ceylon and its Capabilities." London, 1843.

,, "The Fishes of Ceylon." London, 1830.

Cordiner, Jas. "A Description of Ceylon." London, 1807.

Cosmas Indicopleustes. "Description des animaux et des plantes des Indes Orientales." Translated from the Greek of C. I., an Egyptian monk (A.D. 535). London, 1663.

Davy, Dr. J. "An Account of the Interior of Ceylon." Lond., 1821.

Ferguson, A. "Government Railway Extension in Ceylon." Colombo, 1886.

Forbes, J. "The Damboola Cave Temples." Ceylon Almanack, 1834.

,, "Eleven Years in Ceylon," etc. London, 1840.

Haeckel, E. H. P. A. "A Visit to Ceylon." London, 1883.

Hardy, R. S. "Eastern Monachism." London, 1850.

Kelaart, E. F. "Prodromus Faunæ Zeylanicæ." Colombo, 1852-54.

Knighton, Dr. W. "History of Ceylon from the Earliest Period." Edinburgh, 1845.

,, "Tropical Sketches." London, 1855.

,, "Forest Life in Ceylon." London, 1854.

Knox, R. "Historical Relation of the Island of Ceylon, with an Account of the Author's Captivity during Nineteen Years." London, 1681.

Marco Polo. "The Book of Ser Marco Polo," edited by Col. Yule. London, 1871.

Monier-Williams, Sir M. "Buddhism." London, 1889.

Oldenberg, H. "Buddha, sein Leben, seine Lehre, seine Gemeinde." Berlin, 1881.

Percival, Robt. "An Account of the Island of Ceylon." Lond., 1803.

Philalethes (Fellowes, R.) "History of Ceylon to 1815." London, 1817.

Planter, A. "Sport in Ceylon." Colombo, 1888.

R. W. J., a planter. "Ceylon in the Fifties and Eighties." London, 1886.

Ramusio, G. B. "Relation of the Travels of G. Zeno in Persia," etc. Translated by Grey. London, 1873.

Religious Tract Society. "Peeps at Ceylon Life and People." London, 1885.

Ribeiro, Capt. J. "Historical Account of Ceylon," translated from the Portuguese by Dr. J. Harris. London, 1705.

Saint-Hilaire, J. Barthélemy. "Le Bouddha et sa Religion." Paris, 1860.

Selkirk, Rev. J. "Recollections of Ceylon." London, 1844.

Sirr, H. C. "Ceylon and the Cingalese." London, 1850.

Steuart, J. "Account of the Pearl Fisheries of Ceylon," by J. Steuart, Inspector of Fisheries. Colombo, 1843.

Suckling, Capt. H. "Ceylon Ancient and Modern." Lond., 1876.

Tennent, Sir J. E. "Ceylon." London, 1860.

,, "Sketches of Natural History in Ceylon," London, 1861.

Upham, E. "The History and Doctrine of Buddhism." Lond., 1829.

" "The *Mahavansi*," etc., forming the Sacred and Historical Books of Ceylon, translated from the original. London, 1833.

Vincent, Dr. W. "The Commerce and Navigation of the Ancients," by the Very Rev. Dr. Vincent, Dean of Westminster. London, 1800.

The following papers are also well worth reading :—

Asiatic Researches. V. 37. "Travels of a Fakir in Ceylon."

" V. 393. "Narrative of Le Beck."

" VI. 163. "Religion, etc., of the Burmas," by Dr. Buchanan.

" VI. 425. "Narrative of Captain M'Kenzie."

" VII. 399. "The Religion and Manners of Ceylon," by Mr. Joinville.

" X. 126. "The Sacred Isles in the West," by Captain Wilford.

Journal of Asiatic Society of Bengal. VI. 501. "An Examination of Pali Buddhistical Annals," by Hon. G. Turnour.

" " VI. 856. "The Sacred Tooth."

Indian Annual Register for 1799. "Narrative of H. Boyd."

Encyclopædia Britannica. Art. "Ceylon."